STRANGE TALES OF ALE

MARTYN CORNELL

AMBERLEY

First Published 2015

Amberley Publishing
The Hill, Stroud
Gloucestershire, GL5 4EP

www.amberley-books.com

British Library Cataloguing in Publication Data.
A catalogue record for this book is available from the British Library.

ISBN 978 1 4456 4797 5 (hardback)
ISBN 978 1 4456 4808 8 (ebook)

Typeset in 10pt on 13pt Sabon.
Typesetting and Origination by Fakenham Prepress Solutions.
Printed in the UK.

Contents

1	The Great London Beer Flood	5
2	The True History of the Ploughman's Lunch	14
3	Putting Beer in Spitfire Fuel Tanks	21
4	The Bridal Gown – Echo of a Beery Celebration	34
5	The British National Dinner – Roast Beef, Plum Pudding and Ale	40
6	The Potboy in History, Literature and Art	49
7	Dutch Schultz, Beer Hero?	57
8	The True Story Behind Britain's Most Popular Pub Name	63
9	When the Stately Homes of England Drank Twenty-One-Year-Old Ale	68
10	The Tale of the Dimple Beer Mug	82
11	The Dove, Hammersmith – a Tiny Mystery	92
12	The Most Notorious Brewer in History	99
13	The Origins of Binge Drinking	107

14 Havisham's Kentish Ales – Beer in Literature   110

15 In Praise of Rough Pubs   120

16 Give Peas a Chance   123

17 What Shakespeare Drank   130

18 When the Vicar Brewed His Own Beer   136

19 What to Order in a Victorian Public House   141

20 The Brewery that Salami-Sliced Itself to Death   149

21 The Mystery of the Yard of Ale   155

22 The Shadowy History of Sessionability   165

23 Shades, Dives and Other Varieties of British Bar   172

24 Words for Beer   185

25 What Did Pliny the Elder Say About Hops?   201

26 The Patron Saint of English Brewers   206

27 The Jerusalem Tavern, the Trigger's Broom of Pubs   212

28 The Nettle and the Damage Done   220

1

The Great London Beer Flood

If you stand today at the corner of Tottenham Court Road and Oxford Street in the heart of London, surely one of the busiest spots on the planet, crowded with shoppers, tourists and office workers, it is hard to imagine that 200 years ago this was the scene of the Great London Beer Flood. Early in the evening of 17 October 1814, a huge vat filled with maturing porter fell apart at Henry Meux's Horse Shoe brewery, which stood where the Dominion Theatre is now. More than 570 tons of beer crashed through the brewery's back wall and out into the slums behind in a vast wave at least 15 feet high, flooding streets and cellars, smashing into buildings and in at least one case knocking people from a first-floor room. Eight people died, all women and children, and many were injured. It could have been worse. The vat that broke was actually one of the smallest of the seventy or so at the brewery, and contained just under 3,600 barrels of beer. In addition, if the vat had burst an hour or so later, the men of the district would have been home from work and the buildings behind the brewery – all in multiple occupancy, with one family to a room – would have been much fuller when the tsunami of porter hit them.

About the only eyewitness report of what it is like to be hit in the back by a giant wave of beer was written by an anonymous American, who had been unlucky in taking a short-cut down New Street, behind the brewery, when the vat burst.

All at once, I found myself borne onward with great velocity by a torrent which burst upon me so suddenly as almost to deprive me of

Meux's brewery at the bottom of Tottenham Court Road, pictured in 1830, sixteen years after the Great Beer Flood. (Author's collection)

breath. A roar as of falling buildings at a distance, and suffocating fumes, were in my ears and nostrils. I was rescued with great difficulty by the people who immediately collected around me, and from whom I learned the nature of the disaster which had befallen me. An immense vat belonging to a brew house situated in Banbury street [*sic* – now Bainbridge Street], Saint Giles, and containing four or five thousand barrels of strong beer, had suddenly burst and swept everything before it. Whole dwellings were literally riddled by the flood; numbers were killed; and from among the crowds which filled the narrow passages in every direction came the groans of sufferers.

Accounts today of the Meux brewery beer flood are full of claims of 'besotted mobs flinging themselves into gutters full of beer, hampering rescue efforts' and claims that 'many were suffocated in the crush of hundreds trying to get a free beer' and 'the death toll eventually reached 20, including some deaths from alcohol coma'. None of this is borne out by any newspaper reports at the time, nor did newspapers at the time carry stories about riots at the Middlesex Hospital – supposedly because when the victims of the beer flood were taken there, stinking of beer, other patients smelt the porter and thought free drink was being given away – or stories about the floor at the pub where several of the victims' bodies were laid out collapsing under the weight of sightseers and more people being killed. All those tales appear to be completely made up.

In fact, people seem to have behaved very well. Rescuers arrived quickly in great numbers to dig out those buried in the ruins, which included at least one small child, injured but alive. The *Morning Chronicle* wrote in its report of the disaster that 'the cries and groans which issued from the wreckage were dreadful'. Another newspaper, the *Morning Post*, which said the scene behind the brewery resembled the aftermath of an earthquake, commended the 'several Gentlemen' drawn to the spot who were anxious 'to prevent any noise from among the crowd, that the persons who were employed in clearing away the rubbish might ... direct their ears to the ground, in order to discover whether any of the victims were calling for assistance'. It added, 'The caution and humanity with which the labourers proceeded in their distressing task ... deserve warm approbation,' commenting, 'To those that even approached the scene of ruin, the fumes of the beer were very offensive and overpowering.'

Here's an account of the accident from a contemporary journal.

DOMESTIC INTELLIGENCE – DREADFUL ACCIDENT

Monday night, the seventeenth October, one of those accidents which fortunately for the inhabitants of the metropolis is of rare occurrence threw the neighbourhood of St Giles's into the utmost consternation. About six o clock one of the vats in the extensive premises of Messrs Henry Meux and Co in Banbury street St Giles's burst apart; in a moment New street George street and several others in the vicinity were deluged with the contents of 3,555 barrels of strong beer. The fluid in its course swept every thing before it. Two houses in New street adjoining the brew house were totally demolished. The inhabitants, who were of the poorer class, were all at home. In the first floor of one of them a mother and daughter were at tea; the mother was washed out of the window and the daughter was swept away by the current through a partition and dashed to pieces. The back parts of the houses of Mr Goodwin, poulterer, of Mr Hawse, Tavistock Arms, and Nos 24 and 25 in Great Russell street were nearly destroyed. The female servant of the Tavistock Arms was suffocated. Three of Mr Meux's men employed in the brewery were rescued with great difficulty. The site of the place is low and flat, and there being no declivity to carry off the fluid in its fall, it spread and sunk into the neighbouring cellars, all of which were inhabited. Even the cellars in Russell street were inundated and breaches made through the houses. The inhabitants, to save themselves from drowning, had to mount their highest pieces of furniture. The bursting of the brew house walls and the fall of heavy timber materially contributed to aggravate the mischief by forcing the roofs and walls of the adjoining houses. It was feared at first that the lives lost exceeded 20, but we are happy to find the account reduced to eight, whose bodies have been all recovered.

And here's a report of the coroner's inquest:

On Thursday a Coroner's Inquest was held on the dead bodies at St Giles's workhouse. George Crick deposed that he was store house clerk to Messrs H. Meux and Co of the Horse Shoe Brew house in St Giles's, with whom he had lived 17 years. Monday afternoon one of the large iron hoops of the vat which burst fell off. He was not alarmed, as it happened frequently and was not attended by any serious consequence. He wrote to inform a partner, Mr Young, also a vat builder, of the accident, he had the letter in his hand to send to Mr Young, about half past five, half an hour after the accident, and was standing on a platform within three yards of the vat when he heard it burst. He ran to the store house where the vat, was and was shocked to see that one side of the brew house, upwards of 25 feet in height and two bricks and a half thick, with a considerable part of the roof, lay in ruins. The next object that took his attention was his brother, J. Crick, who was a superintendent under him, lying senseless, he being pulled from under one of the butts. He and the labourer were now in the Middlesex Hospital. An hour after, witness found the body of Ann Saville floating among the butts, and also part of a private still, both of which floated from neighbouring houses. The cellar and two deep wells in it were full of beer, which witness and those about him endeavoured to save, so that they could not go to see the accident, which happened outwardly. The height of the vat that burst was 22 feet; it was filled within 4 inches of the top and then contained 3555 barrels of entire, being beer that was ten months brewed; the four inches would hold between 30 and 40 barrels more; the hoop which burst was 700 cwt, which was the least weight of any of 22 hoops on the vat. There were seven large hoops, each of which weighed near a ton. When the vat burst the force and pressure was so great that it stove several hogsheads of porter and also knocked the cock out of a vat nearly as large that was in the cellar or regions below; this vat contained 2100 barrels all of which except 800 barrel also ran; about they lost in all between 8 and 9000 barrels of beer; the vat from whence the cock was knocked out ran about a barrel a minute; the vat that burst had been built between eight and nine years and was kept always nearly full. It had an opening on the top about a yard square; it was about eight inches from the wall; witness supposes it was the rivets of the hoops that slipped, none of the hoops being broke and the foundation where the vat stood not giving way. The beer was old, so that the accident could not have been occasioned by the fermentation, that natural process being past; besides, the action would then have been upwards and thrown off the flap made moveable for that purpose.

Richard Hawes deposed that he lived at No 22 Great Russell street Bloomsbury, the Tavistock Arms Public house; about half past five o' clock on Monday evening witness was in his tap room when he heard the crash; the back part of his house was beaten in and every thing in his cellar destroyed; the cellar and tap room filled with beer so that it was pouring across the street into the areas on the opposite side; the deceased, Eleanor Cooper, his servant, was in the yard washing pots at the time the accident happened; she was buried under the ruins, from whence she was dug out about 10 minutes past eight o' clock; she was found standing by the water butt, quite dead.

John Cummins deposed that he was a bricklayer and lived in Pratt's place, Camden Town, being the owner of some houses in New street where the principal part of the persons who were lost, resided; he attended on the spot all day on Tuesday to render assistance to the sufferers. Elizabeth Smith, a bricklayer's wife, was the first body they found, about twelve o'clock in the ruins of a first floor. Sarah Bates, a child, was discovered in about an hour afterward in the ruins of No 3 New street. Catharine Butler, a widow, Mary Mulvey and her son Thomas Murry, a boy three years of age, were found about four o clock, on Tuesday afternoon. Hannah Banfield, a girl about four years and a half old, with her mother and another child, were at tea on the first floor; the two former were washed by the flood into the ruins; the dead body of Hannah Banfield was found in the ruins about half past six; the mother was carried to the Middlesex Hospital, and the last mentioned child was found nearly suffocated in a bed in the room.

The Jury without hesitation, returned a Verdict of Died by Casualty Accidentally and by Misfortune.

Why did they store such huge quantities of porter – the strong, black beer that was the most popular in London at the time – in such enormous vessels? Experience had shown that porter stored for months in vats acquired a particularly sought-after set of flavours, and storing it in really big vessels reduced the risk of oxidisation (since the surface area merely squared as the volume cubed). This 'stale' (meaning 'stood for some time', rather than 'off'), flat and probably quite sour aged porter was then sent out in casks when ready, and mixed at the time of service in the pub with porter from a cask that was 'mild' – that is, fresh and still lively, and probably a little sweet. Customers would specify the degree of mildness or staleness they would like their porter, having it mixed to their own preference.

The vat that burst, in spite of all the death and destruction it caused, was far from the largest at the brewery. Indeed, this report from a visit to the Horse Shoe Brewery in 1812, two years before the disaster, written by a thirty-four-year-old Orkney-born novelist called Mrs Mary Brunton, suggests it was one of the smallest.

In Meux's Brewery every thing is as filthy as steam and smoke, and dust and rust can make it; except the steam engine, which is as polished and as clean as the bars of a drawing-room grate. The first operation of this engine is to stir the malt in vats of twenty-eight feet diameter, filled with boiling water; the second is, in due time, to raise the wort to the coolers, in the floor above; then this wort is conveyed by leaden pipes into the tub where it is to ferment, and afterwards into the casks where the porter is first deposited. One of these casks, which I saw, measures seventy feet in diameter, and is said to have cost £10,000; the iron hoops on it weigh eighty tons; and we were told that it actually contained, when we saw it, 18,000 barrels, or £40,000 worth of porter. Another contained 16,000 barrels, and from thence to 4,000; there are above seventy casks in the store.

From the top of the immense building, which holds this vast apparatus, we had a complete view of London and the adjacent country. I must own, however, that I was rejoiced to find myself once more safe in the street … I never feel myself in a very elevated situation, without being seized with an universal tremor. I shook in every limb for an hour after coming down.

On the Friday after the disaster, the *Morning Post* was able to report that, 'by strict enquiry of the different beadles, and at the public houses to a late hour', it could state that no other lives had been lost in the accident besides the eight on whom the inquest had been held. Five more victims, 'some of whom are dreadfully bruised', were still in the Middlesex Hospital: George Crick's brother John; Patrick Murphy, a labourer at the brewery; Mary Banfield; and two children 'who were picked up in a state of suffocation and much bruised'. Spectators were still arriving to see the devastation. 'The numbers who were led to view the spot during the whole of yesterday, was beyond calculation,' the *Post* said, momentarily forgetting subject-verb number agreement. The five who died at the New Street cellar wake were waked themselves, in the parlour at the Ship pub in Bainbridge Street, on the south side of the brewery, while the coffins of the other three victims were laid out in a nearby yard.

If the accident had happened just an hour later, the *Morning Post* commented, 'Many more lives would have been lost, as the men would have been home from work, and the cellar in which the wake was held would have been full, as is customary among the Irish.' All those who came to see the bodies were asked to make a small donation – sixpence or a shilling – towards the families of the survivors, with the collection at the Ship totalling £33 5s 7d. It was not much, against estimates that the poor victims of the flood had lost £3,000 in ruined belongings. A fund was set up for their relief by the churchwardens of the two parishes that covered the area hit by the disaster, St Giles's and St George, Bloomsbury; within a month, more than £800 had been raised, including £30 from Florance Young (whose family later owned Young's brewery in Wandsworth).

Initial estimates for the amount of lost beer was 8,000 to 9,000 barrels, getting on for 10 per cent of total yearly production, though the final calculation came to only 7,664 barrels of porter. Meux and Co. claimed their estimate total loss to be £23,000 'at the lowest calculation', equivalent, on a share-of-GDP calculation, to more than £66 million today. The firm petitioned Parliament for a refund of the duty it had paid on the lost beer, and the malt and hops that went into it. An Act was passed the following year that allowed the partners to brew, duty free, an amount equivalent in duties to the duty on the beer lost, which saved them around £7,250.

The Horse Shoe brewery maintained its position as one of London's leading porter producers for the rest of the nineteenth century; indeed, it was the last one to remain solely a porter brewer, with production of ale not being introduced until 1872. But tastes changed over the nineteenth century, 'stale' porter fell out of favour, and by the 1890s the big vats were being dismantled; the oak they were made from was recycled into pub bar-tops. Quite possibly there are pubs in London now whose bars are made out of old porter vats.

The Meux (pronounced 'mewks') brewery stood at the corner of Tottenham Court Road and Oxford Street until the early 1920s, but it was increasingly an anachronism as a large brewery in the heart of London, and production was shifted in 1921 to a brewery in Nine Elms in South West London (itself now demolished and the site of New Covent Garden flower and vegetable market), while the Horse Shoe brewery was replaced by the Dominion Theatre. The Horseshoe Inn next door remained open until the 1990s or so, but eventually closed; you can still get a drink on the site, as a bistro now occupies the ground floor, but you cannot, alas, get a pint of porter.

2

The True History of the Ploughman's Lunch

For quite some years the Ploughman's Lunch, that simple bar snack of bread, cheese and pickle (plus some lettuce and a sliced tomato, if you like), has stood accused of representing the worst kind of British fakery. The Ploughman's Lunch has been charged with masquerading as a false representation of simpler times, when muscular farm workers furrowed the fields with the aid of a couple of tons of Clydesdale or Shire, while in reality, it has been claimed, it's the invention of Italian-suited marketers in slick Soho offices. Is this true? And what does the father of Martin Bell, the BBC journalist and former MP for Tatton, have to do with the story?

The accusations of fraud and pretence were flung at what was already a staple of the British pub menu by the British novelist Ian McEwan in the screenplay he wrote for the film called *The Ploughman's Lunch* in 1982. The pivotal scene occurs when the journalist anti-hero, James Penfield, played by Jonathan Pryce as a creep who would sell his grandmother if it would advance his career, meets a television advert director, Matthew Fox, played by Frank Finlay, in a pub for a chat:

MATTHEW: I'll tell you another thing. We might have led the world once into the Industrial Revolution, now we lead with television commercials. We're the best, it's as simple as that. Even the Americans will admit it now ... the camera work, the acting, the scripts, special effects. We've got the lot. Nearly all the good directors here have ambitions to make serious films. (A sudden laugh.) That food you're eating.

The Ploughman's Lunch, not an invention of 1960s admen sitting in Soho, but a genuine country tradition. (Author's collection)

JAMES: Yes.

MATTHEW: What would you call it?

JAMES: I dunno. Ploughman's Lunch.

MATTHEW: Ploughman's Lunch. Traditional English fare.

JAMES: Uhuh.

MATTHEW: In fact it's the invention of an advertising campaign they ran in the early sixties to encourage people to eat in pubs. A completely successful fabrication of the past, the Ploughman's Lunch was.

We look at James's plate, the unappetising food. Matthew takes a long drink.

What the Ploughman's Lunch represented in *The Ploughman's Lunch*, which was directed by Richard Eyre and came out in 1983, the year after the Falklands War, was explained by the film and theatre critic Benjamin Nightingale in an article in the *New York Times* in 1984.

> In every other British pub these days you can buy something called a Ploughman's Lunch. It consists of bread, butter, chutney and a slice of cheese, and might at first glance or bite seem just the sort of meal generations of farm-laborers carried in their knapsacks, as they plodded through the furrows. But that yeomanly picnic, name and all, was actually invented by marketing experts in the 1960s. Some pubs tacitly admit as much by wrapping the butter in glossy paper and putting the cheese and chutney in little cellophane containers. The Ploughman's Lunch is a fraud and a con – and as such, Richard Eyre would suggest, an extremely dense metaphor for Britain itself, which is still creating fictions about the past and using them to suit the needs of the present.

So is the Ploughman's Lunch a con? As an expression, it appears to be surprisingly modern. Until 2005, the earliest reference the Oxford English Dictionary could find to the name was from 1970, in the foreword to a book called *The Cheese Handbook*, where Richard Trehane, then chairman of the English Country Cheese Council, declared, 'English cheese and beer have for centuries formed a perfect combination enjoyed as the Ploughman's Lunch.'

Trehane, himself the son of a dairy farmer, was correct in declaring the antiquity of cheese and beer as a combination – references to the two together go back to at least medieval times – and implying their agricultural connection. In 1801, Arthur Bryant described the food given to Hertfordshire harvest workers as 'at six o'clock bread, cheese and ale; at nine a hot breakfast; between eleven and twelve, bread and cheese; they dine at half past one, and have beef or mutton, and plumb-pudding; at four in the afternoon they have cheese and ale again

... and at night they have a hot supper in the farmhouse.'

But the cheese and ale in that prodigious consumption of calories was a harvest worker's early breakfast, elevenses and late-afternoon snack, not a 'ploughman's lunch'. In 1934, when the anonymous author of *A Book about Beer* wrote about beer and cheese, he said, 'Good bread, good cheese and good beer provide a complete meal which the most elaborate meal can scarcely better. Bread and cheese, indeed, form a perfect background for a beer of good quality. They set off its smoothness, its gulpability, its essential rotundity.' But he never called the combination a 'ploughman's lunch'.

When Andrew Campbell wrote *The Book of Beer* in 1956, he declared, in a chapter on beer with food, that 'the classic British snack lunch consists of bread, cheese and beer, and if accompanied by a little celery, lettuce or other salad, or followed by some fresh fruit, is dietetically a meal for a king ... it is a very sensitive matter to get the right [beer] for the cheese ... Draught Bass and good farmhouse Cheddar; Guinness goes well with Cheshire, Lancashire or Wensleydale.' He never mentioned ploughmen, either.

In 2005, 'Ploughman's Lunch' was one of the expressions the Oxford English Dictionary asked the public to help it out with in the BBC programme *Balderdash and Piffle*. As a result of evidence offered by former Milk Marketing Board staffers, the researchers for the programme found minutes of a meeting of the Milk Marketing Board in November 1960 that included a mention of budgetary provision for printing 5,000 'Ploughman's Lunch showcards' for distributing round pubs. This led the BBC to declare, 'Documents uncovered at the National Archive from the Milk Marketing Board reveal that the Ploughman's Lunch was invented as a marketing ploy to sell British cheese in pubs.'

So – Ploughman's Lunch, guilty as charged, then; nothing but a cynical 1960s marketing man's invention to offload more cheese.

However, the evidence to set the Ploughman's Lunch free from the accusations of fraud was out there all along, albeit in the pages of an extremely obscure magazine called *A Monthly*

Bulletin, produced by the old Brewers' Society between the 1930s and the early 1970s. The July 1956 edition has a report of the activities of the Cheese Bureau, which 'exists for the admirable purpose of popularising cheese and, as a corollary, the public house lunch of bread, beer, cheese and pickles. This traditional combination was broken by rationing; the Cheese Bureau hopes, by demonstrating the natural affinity of the two parties, to effect a remarriage.' The magazine reported a tasting held at the Samson and Hercules in Norwich (a dancehall rather than a pub), and 'that good countryman, Mr Adrian Bell, writer and broadcaster (and above all, author of *Corduroy*) pronounced the blessing.'

It is a sign of the fickleness of fame that no explanation as to the nature of Bell's book *Corduroy* was felt necessary in 1956, while today the author is effectively unknown. Bell was the son of a Fleet Street editor who had turned to farming, combined with journalism and book-writing. *Corduroy* had been written in 1930, but in 1940 it was brought out as a Penguin paperback in just the size to fit into a kitbag or a uniform pocket, and its evocation of a rural, peaceful England of farms, seasons and harvests spoke to the sentiments and ambitions of servicemen across all theatres of war. To quote Adrian's son, Martin Bell, the former BBC war correspondent, the book 'provided a life-line to another world, a world of peace and sanity, of enduring values and country rhythms remote from the war's destruction'. To an audience barely a decade away from the end of the war, the book needed no introduction. At the tasting in Norwich, Adrian Bell 'made a spirited plea for the 'auld alliance' of beer and cheese', and went on to say that he recollected his ploughman 'eating lunch, with a connoisseur's palate, in a Suffolk barn, and old days of rabbiting in the snow, when the party drank beer and ate bread and cheese'.

Bell then called upon more pubs to provide bread and cheese at lunchtime, and said, 'There's a pub quite close to where I live where ... all you need say is, "Ploughboy's Lunch, Harry, please." And in a matter of minutes a tray is handed across the counter to you on which is a good square hunk of bread, a lump of butter and a wedge of cheese, and pickled onions, along with your pint of beer. "Ploughboy's Lunch", that's called – remember those words: they stand for something pretty good.'

That was 'Plough*boy's* Lunch', rather than 'Plough*man's*', of course. But a year later, the June 1957 edition of *A Monthly Bulletin* reported on another tasting by the Cheese Bureau, this time at Fishmonger's Hall in London in conjunction with the Brewers' Company, to encourage 'the traditional public house meal of bread, beer, cheese and pickles'. Some 500 guests, the magazine said, tried out sixteen different types of cheese 'and beer brewed by eight firms – all of which, incidentally, have been household names in London for 150 years or more' (pause for a quiet weep at the fact that, six decades on, only one of those brewers is still making beer in London). After the tasting 'there followed a "Ploughman's Lunch" of cottage bread, cheese, lettuce, hard-boiled eggs, cold sausages and, of course, beer. This is just the sort of light mid-day meal that one might expect to find in an ordinary public house, where the customers do not wish to spend much time or much money on their lunch, and where the landlord cannot afford a catering staff. Licensed victuallers please note.'

This appears to be the real first mention of the expression 'Ploughman's Lunch', predating the *OED*'s previous earliest mention by all of three years and five months. It looks as if the Cheese Bureau had picked up on Bell's use of the phrase 'Ploughboy's Lunch' at the Norwich tasting and decided that, by changing 'boy' to 'man' and thus making the meal sound more muscular and adult, it had the ideal name with which to promote cheese-based snacks in public houses. However, the nomenclature was not yet completely settled. In April 1958, the following year, *The Times* brought out a supplement on 'Beer in Britain', to which Adrian Bell (who was the first crossword compiler for the newspaper) contributed a piece on food in pubs that included the sentence, 'In a certain inn to-day you have only to say, "Ploughboy's Lunch, please," and for a shilling there is bread and cheese and pickled onions to go with your pint, and make a meal seasoned with gossip, and not solitary amid a multitude.' Two years later, however, in 1960, when the supplement was issued as a book, the words 'Ploughboy's Lunch, please' had been altered to 'Plough*man*'s Lunch, please' (my emphasis). Had the Cheese Board been on to *The Times* and said, 'We don't call it Ploughboy's Lunch, it's Ploughman's Lunch, thanks, old chap.'?

Probably. But the evidence from Adrian Bell, and *A Monthly Bulletin*, is that bread, cheese and pickles was a genuine 'traditional public house meal' from at least before the Second World War, which had been knocked on the head by wartime rationing of staples such as cheese, and that bread, cheese and pickles was something genuinely consumed by ploughmen – or ploughboys – for their lunch. The dish wasn't invented by marketing men in the 1960s, but revived by the Cheese Board, representatives of Britain's cheese makers, in the 1950s, and the name Ploughman's Lunch might be marketing flannel but it seems to have its roots in authenticity. Ian McEwan and Richard Eyre were making false accusations. The Ploughman's Lunch is innocent.

3

Putting Beer in Spitfire Fuel Tanks

Normandy, summer 1944, and one of the biggest concerns of the British troops who have made it over the channel, survived the landings and pushed out into the bocage against bitter German resistance is not the V-1-flying-bomb blitz threatening their families back home, nor the continued failure to capture the port of Cherbourg. It is the lack of beer in the bridgehead. On 20 June 1944, two weeks after D-Day, Reuter's special correspondent with the Allied Forces in France wrote to newspapers in the UK that all that was available in the newly liberated estaminets a few miles inland from the beaches was cider, 'and it is pretty watery stuff. I saw a British private wistfully order a pint of mild and bitter: but the glass he sat down with contained the eternal cider.'

It would not be until 12 July that 'real British beer' finally officially reached the battling troops in Normandy, and the quantity was enough only for one pint per man. But long before then, enterprising pilots in the RAF – and the USAAF – had been engaged in shipping beer into Northern France privately, using what the troops called 'flying pubs'.

Some of the first attempts to bring beer over the Channel after D-Day used the expendable drop tanks, or jettison tanks, to give them their proper RAF designation, carried by aircraft such as the Spitfire and Typhoon and normally filled with fuel to give them extra range. These seem to have been semi-official efforts: the Air Ministry actually distributed a photograph to newspapers showing a Spitfire of 332 (Norwegian) Squadron at Tangmere airfield in Sussex having a 45-gallon jettison tank being filled with beer from two wooden casks supplied by the Chichester

Tangmere, Sussex, July 1944. In front of a Spitfire IX of 332 (Norwegian)
Squadron, a standard 45 gallon Typhoon/Hurricane 'Torpedo' jettison tank,
modified for use on the Spitfire (because of an expected shortage of 45 gallon
shaped or slipper tanks), is filled with PA ale for flying over to Normandy,
while an RAF 'erk' writes a cheery message on the tank. (Picture courtesy of
Shepherd Neame Ltd)

brewer Henty & Constable, while the pilot relaxed on the wing
and an RAF 'erk' (member of the ground staff) wrote a cheery
message on the tank. (The pilot in the photograph, incidentally,
who was wearing a Norwegian Army Airforce cap badge, was
almost certainly the Norwegian Spitfire ace Wing Commander
Rolf Arne Berg, CO of No. 132 Norwegian Wing, who was
killed a few months later in February 1945, aged twenty-seven,
while attacking a German airfield in the Netherlands.)

It was presumably 270 gallons of beer from Henty and
Constable that was flown in drop tanks slung under three
Spitfire Mk IXbs from Tangmere to an airfield at Bény-Sur-
Mer in Normandy, some 110 miles south of England and
3 miles from the sea, on June 13 1944, D-Day plus seven
– the first known landing of beer during the invasion. One

of the pilots was Flight Lieutenant Lloyd Berryman of 412 Squadron, 126 Wing, Second Tactical Air Force, Royal Canadian Air Force. The airstrip at Bény-Sur-Mer was not, in fact, to be finished officially for another two days when Berryman's boss, Wing Commander Keith Hudson, singled him out at a briefing at the wing's Tangmere base to deliver a 'sizeable' beer consignment to the airstrip, known as B4. Berryman recalled,

The instructions went something like this, 'Get a couple other pilots and arrange with the officers' mess to steam out the jet [jettison] tanks and load them up with beer. When we get over the beachhead drop out of formation and land on the strip. We're told the Nazis are fouling the drinking water, so it will be appreciated. There's no trouble finding the strip, the battleship Rodney is firing salvoes on Caen and it's immediately below. We'll be flying over at 13,000 [feet] so the beer will be cold enough when you arrive.'

I remember getting Murray Haver from Hamilton and a third pilot (whose name escapes me) to carry out the caper. In reflection it now seems like an appropriate Air Force gesture for which the erks (infantrymen) would be most appreciative. By the time I got down to 5,000 the welcoming from the Rodney was hardly inviting, but sure enough, there was the strip. Wheels down and in we go, three Spits with 90-gallon jet tanks fully loaded with cool beer.

As I rolled to the end of the mesh runway it was hard to figure … there was absolutely no one in sight. What do we do now, I wondered, we can't just sit here and wait for someone to show up. What's with the communications? Finally I saw someone peering out at us from behind a tree and I waved frantically to get him out to the aircraft. Sure enough out bounds this army type and he climbs onto the wing with the welcome: 'What the hell are you doing here?' Whereupon he got a short, but nevertheless terse, version of the story.

'Look,' he said, 'can you see that church steeple at the far end of the strip? Well it's loaded with German snipers and we've been all day trying to clear them out so you better drop your tanks and bugger off before it's too late.' In moments we were out of there, but such was the welcoming for the first Spitfire at our B4 airstrip in Normandy.

Later, in the 1950s back in Canada, by chance Berryman actually met the man who climbed onto his wing and told him to bugger off.

Four days after Berryman's landing, on 17 June 1944, and eleven days after the invasion started, a Spitfire of 416 Squadron, Royal Canadian Air Force, flew over from England to the newly built airfield at Bazenville, just 3 miles from Gold Beach, with a drop tank full of beer slung below its fuselage. The tank had been scoured out first with steam, but 'tough luck; it still tasted of petrol', according to Dan Noonan, a Flight Commander with 416 Squadron.

The heftier Hawker Typhoon could carry even more beer. Pilots of the RAF's 123 Wing, flying rocket-firing Typhoons and based from 19 July 1944 at Martragny, a few miles east of Bayeux, would run a 'shufti-kite' across to Shoreham, 110 miles away, where a local brewery would fill two 90-gallon jettison tanks attached below each of the Typhoon's wings with beer. Then the pilot would hurry back across the Channel and the RAF personnel at Martragny would drink it, quickly. There was one problem with transporting beer in jettison tanks: according to 123 Wing's commanding officer, the New Zealand-born RAF ace Group Captain Desmond Scott, on the trip over to Normandy the beer 'took on rather a metallic taste, but the wing made short work of it'.

However, the journey over the channel, at 15,000 feet or so, cooled the beer down nicely for when it reached those on the ground. Indeed, according to newspaper reports, not only did Spitfires supply beer shortly after D-Day in jettison tanks made from vulcanised paper fibre, but P-47 Thunderbolt fighters, presumably flown by the USAAF, had carried iced custard, or ice-cream, in their drop-tanks to troops on the Normandy beachheads. 'They flew at 15,000 feet and delivered their cargo iced in perfect condition.' (This is not as unlikely as it seems; the US army had mobile ice-cream making machines for the troops in the Second World War, and so did many US Navy ships.)

The Typhoons' exploits were reported in *Time* Magazine on 2 July 1944 under the headline 'Flying Pubs'.

> A great thirst attacked British troops rushing emergency landing strips to completion in the dust of Normandy. Thinking of luckier comrades guzzling in country estaminets and town bistros, the runway builders began to grouse. They wanted beer. They got it. Rocket-firing Typhoons, before going on to shoot up Nazis, landed on the runways with auxiliary fuel tanks full of beer. Swarms of the thirsty gathered round with enamel mugs. The first tank-fulls tasted bad because of the tank linings; this flavor was overcome by chemical means and later loads were delicious. Just like the corner pub at home.

Unfortunately, United States Army Air Forces P-47 Thunderbolts did for 123 Wing's beer runs. The Typhoon was easily mistaken by inexperienced American pilots for the German Focke-Wulf Fw190 fighter, and according to Group Captain Scott, 'Our aerial brewer's dray was attacked by American Thunderbolts twice in one day, and was forced to jettison its beer tanks into the Channel ... beer cost us money, and these two encounters proved expensive.' The Wing's draught beer flights came to a sudden halt, and Scott had to arrange for an old twin-engined Anson to fly in cases of Guinness. 'The troops mixed it with champagne to produce black velvet. It was hardly a cockney's drink, but they appeared to like it', he wrote.

It may have been 123 Wing's experience that was covered in a publication called *The Airman's Almanac* in 1945.

> A possible peacetime use for the auxiliary fuel tanks attached to the underside of fighter planes in World War II to increase their range was demonstrated in the Normandy invasion of

1944. British ground crews, rushing emergency landing strips to completion in the dust and heat of the French province, complained of thirst. Their complaint being heard, rocket-firing Typhoons coming over from England on their way to German targets landed on the newly built strips with their military fuel tanks full of beer. The first tankfuls tasted awful because of the tank linings. Before the second 'beer trip' the tanks were treated chemically and the air-hauled brew was reported extremely palatable.

Ironically, Thunderbolt pilots learnt what the Typhoons had been doing, and copied it themselves. Lieutenant William R. Dunn of the 13th Fighter Squadron, USAAF, the first American air ace of the Second World War, was a P-47 Thunderbolt pilot in Normandy. He recorded, 'During our brief stay at A6 airfield, we learned another trick of the trade from our neighbouring RAF allies, a Typhoon squadron based near Caen. Periodically they'd send a kite with a clean belly tank back to England, where the tank was filled with beer. A flight back to France at an altitude of about 15,000 feet and the beer arrived nice and cold. We soon followed their lead, with our 150-gallon belly tanks. Those British types sure know how to take all the comforts of home to war with them.'

The other method used was to attach casks to the bomb racks. Pilots with the RAF's No. 131 (Polish) wing, flying Spitfire Mk IXs (probably 302 Squadron or 308 Squadron, both fighter-bomber units), claimed to have invented the idea of the 'beer bomb', using casks that had homemade nose-cones fitted to make them more streamlined, which were fitted to the Spitfire's bomb racks. On 3 August 1944 131 Wing moved from England to the airfield at Plumentot, near Caen, and 'beer bombing' began. According to the book *Destiny Can Wait: the Polish Air Force in the Second World War,* Polish members of the RAF made several ingenious inventions.

One of the most popular was a shower-bath system manufactured out of empty petrol tins. Even more popular was the 'beer-bomb', invented and first used by No. 131 Fighter Wing when still stationed in England. The bomb has nothing atomic about it, so the details can now be divulged. The invention is, in fact, simplicity itself: it entailed a barrel of beer, a bomb-carrying aircraft, and a willing pilot (the three were available in increasing order of magnitude). The procedure, freely disclosed for the benefit of thirsty humanity, was for the aircraft to be carefully 'bombed up' with a barrel of beer, flown off with every precaution to Plumentot in Normandy and landed with equal care. Never were bombs more warmly welcomed. Not least because of the dust.

Pictures exist of the 'beer bombs' being put together; this was presumably at Ford airfield in West Sussex, where 302 and 308 Squadrons were based just before they were moved to Plumentot. If this were the case, again, the beer may well have come from Henty and Constable, eight or so miles away at Chichester.

One Kentish brewery that apparently supplied beer for transport across by fighter plane was Bushell, Watkins & Smith, of the Black Eagle brewery in Westerham. According to Westerham villager Edward 'Ted' Turner,

> I worked at a garage called Brittain's Engineering in Peckham in London making Bailey bridges for sending to France for the invasion ... We were also making 'jettison' auxiliary fuel tanks for fighter planes to carry extra fuel to enable them to fly further into Europe and still get back home. Once refuelling facilities were established over there, the Westerham brewery used to fill those auxiliary non-returnable petrol tanks with Westerham ales for our troops in Europe. Black Eagle lorries delivered it in barrels to Biggin Hill [four miles from Westerham] where the auxiliary dual-purpose tanks were filled with Bitter on one side and Mild on the other. We made them of 16 gauge metal with baffles for safe landing, the RAF's version of the brewer's dray.

There is also a photograph of a cask at the Black Eagle brewery with a sign on it declaring, 'This Cask containing "Westerham" Bitter was flown to France 'D' day, June 6th 1944, by the

Royal Air Force.' Unfortunately, there are problems with the Westerham claims. The three fighter squadrons that had been using the airfield departed in late April 1944 for Tangmere, where they would be closer to the Normandy beaches. In any case, Biggin Hill was abandoned by the RAF soon after the Normandy landings. On 13 June 1944, V-1 'doodlebug' flying-bomb attacks on London began, and Biggin Hill – right in the V-1s' flightpath – was deemed too dangerous to continue to be used by aircraft, with Balloon Command taking the airfield over as part of the line of barrage balloons put up against the V-1s. Flying operations did not begin again at Biggin Hill until September 1944, and fighter aircraft do not seem to have returned until October. However, one of the squadrons that had been based at Biggin Hill until April 1944 was 412 Squadron, which had made that first 'drop-tank beer delivery' to Normandy from Tangmere on June 13. It is possible that the beer in the tanks might have come from the Westerham brewery, 50 miles away, which the pilots of 412 would have known very well.

Certainly, pilots were happy to fly long distances to pick up beer. Thorsteinn 'Tony' Jonsson, the only Icelander to join the RAF, was flying North American Aviation P-51 Mustang III fighter-bombers with 65 Squadron, based at Ford, when the D-Day invasion began. On June 27 his squadron moved to the temporary airfield at Martragny, designated B7, 5 miles from Bayeux and only some 2,000 yards from the German lines. However, Jonsson recorded,

Life in our camp was really quite pleasant and comfortable. Admittedly we missed the luxury of being able to pop into a pub at the end of a day's work for a pint of beer, and to mix with the ladies that were usually to be found there to add spice to our existence. At the beginning of the invasion and for the next few weeks, beer was severely rationed in Normandy ... But some bright lad in our Wing had an excellent brain-wave; why not bring beer over from England in the large auxiliary tanks that could be hung under the wings of our Mustangs? Each tank could hold 75 gallons – this would make an excellent addition to our meagre ration. Action was immediately taken.

Four tanks were sent to a factory for their insides to be coated with a substance to prevent the taste of metal, as is done with preserving cans, and taps were fitted. A contract was made with a brewery in London, and on an appointed day every week a Mustang flew with two empty 'beer' tanks to Croydon aerodrome and brought back two full ones; one containing mild and the other bitter. These tanks were placed on trestles in our mess-tent, which quickly became known as the best pub in Normandy. It did not take long for the word to spread to nearby military units that we had a good supply of beer, and our mess was frequently a very popular and crowded place in the evenings. The fact that nurses from a military hospital in the neighbourhood were regulars only helped to boost the attendance ... It was not long before the beer trips were increased to two a week. Although most pilots like to nip over to England whenever possible, to contact families and loved ones, the beer-run was not in demand. The reason was that a full beer tank could easily fall off if the landing was not perfectly smooth. The 'beer kite's' arrival was watched by all available personnel, and woe to the poor pilot who was unlucky enough to bounce!

It was 150 miles from Martragny to Croydon (at the time the main airfield in London), making the 'beer run' for 65 Squadron a 300-mile round trip. Croydon's one brewery at the time was Page & Overton, a subsidiary of Charrington's brewery in Mile End, and it was presumably Page & Overton's mild and bitter that flew back in the tanks of the Mustangs.

Confirmation that Henty & Constable supplied much of the beer to arrive in Normandy after D-Day comes from Jeffrey Quill, chief test pilot at Vickers, the parent company of Supermarine, maker of the Spitfire. Quill recalled,

After D-Day in 1944, there was a problem about getting beer over to the Normandy airfields. Henty and Constable (the Sussex brewers) were happy to make the stuff available at the

83 Group Support Unit at Ford, near Littlehampton. For some inexplicable reason, however, beer had a low priority rating on the available freight aircraft. So we adapted Spitfire bomb racks so that an 18-gallon barrel could be carried under each wing of the Spitfires which were being ferried across from Ford to Normandy on a daily basis.

We were, in fact, a little concerned about the strength situation of the barrels, and on application to Henty and Constables for basic stressing data we were astonished to find that the eventuality of being flown on the bomb racks of a Spitfire was a case which had not been taken into consideration in the design of the barrels. However, flight tests proved them to be up to the job. This installation, incidentally, was known as Mod XXX Depth charge.

According to one source with a slightly different spin on the story, the job of designing fittings that would secure the kilderkins to the Spitfire's bomb racks was done at High Post airfield, Salisbury, one of the final assembly centres for Spitfire manufacture, 'more or less as a joke'. The plan to put beer in long-range tanks was abandoned 'when it was found later that the practice contaminated fuel, so Strong's, the Romsey brewers, supplied complete barrels of Triple "X". This modification was given a fictitious number to conceal the operation from more official or officious eyes.'

There was already a link between Strong's and Spitfires. After the Luftwaffe bombed Vickers-Supermarine's headquarters in 1940, the company's design and administration offices were transferred to Hursley Park, Winchester, a magnificent mansion requisitioned after the death that same year of its owner, Sir George Cooper, chairman of Strong's. That Strong's certainly was involved in the supply of casks to be carried on Spitfire bomb racks is confirmed by the existence of a photograph of just such a cask slung under a Spitfire wing, clearly branded 'STRONG ROMSEY'.

The hint that Quill gave about the 'flying drays' being replacement Spitfires ferried across to squadrons on the

Normandy front line from England is given extra support by a
newspaper story from the middle of August 1944.

> With beer in their bomb racks, replacement Typhoons from
> England are sure of a specially boisterous welcome from the
> thirsty troops in Normandy. For the beer shortage is just as acute
> over there as it is in England. So at least one Typhoon squadron
> has solved its problem by importing its own beer. Whenever a
> replacement aircraft flies to Normandy the pilot takes a quantity
> of beer, carrying it in nine-gallon barrels with special streamlined
> nose fittings slung in the bomb racks. This system has been found
> to be much better than the original method of taking the beer in
> petrol tanks, which gave the beer a nasty flavour. In the event of
> the pilot running into trouble, the barrels are jettisoned as if they
> were bombs. Then another kind of trouble awaits him at the end
> of his journey.

Wing Commander Johnnie Johnson had landed on D-Day plus
three with his 127 Wing, two squadrons of Canadians, at a
newly built airfield at St Croix-sur-Mer designated B3, just over
a mile and a half from the landing beaches. After several days
of tinned 'compo' rations, Johnson sent a note to his favourite
Sussex landlord, Arthur King, at the Unicorn in Chichester,
asking for help. Every day, a twin-engined Anson flew into St
Croix from Tangmere with mail, newspapers and spare parts,
and King arranged for items such as tomatoes, fresh lobsters,
newly baked bread and 'a reasonable supply of stout' to be
carried across in the Anson with the mail.

When news of the arrangement leaked into the newspapers,
King was visited by someone from Customs and Excise, who
warned him that if he carried on, he would need an export
licence. However, Johnson recorded in his memoirs,

> Since its introduction to the Service in 1939, the versatile Spitfire
> had participated in many diverse roles ... Now it fulfilled yet
> another role, perhaps not so vital as some of the tasks it had
> undertaken in the past, but to us of supreme importance. Back in

England some ingenious mind had modified the bomb racks slung
under each wing so that a small barrel of beer could be carried
instead of a 500-pound bomb. Daily, this modern version of the
brewers' dray flew across the Channel and alighted at St Croix.
The beer suffered no ill effects from its unorthodox journey and
was more than welcome in our mess.

Johnson's memoir of the war, *Wing Leader*, included a photograph
of a Spitfire IX in D-Day black-and-white stripes carrying a
kilderkin of beer slung from each bomb rack, captioned, 'Our
version of the brewer's dray.' This seems to have given rise to
the myth that the picture is of Johnson's own Spitfire. But the
photograph in the book is credited to Vickers Armstrong, and
is almost certainly one of the aircraft manufacturer's publicity
shots, and nothing to do with Johnson.

Eventually, organised supplies of beer for the troops supplanted
the 'flying drays'. In November 1944, the government actually
ruled that supplies of beer for troops overseas should equal 5 per
cent of total national production, meaning all stronger 'export'
beers, all naturally conditioned beers with a life of six weeks or
more and all beers that could be pasteurised had to be put in the
hands of the forces' catering service, the Naafi. At the same time,
breweries in liberated areas of France were being put to use to
make beer for the troops.

By then it was the turn of the Home Front to be short of
beer, however. Brewers blamed a shortage of labour, saying the
women workers who had replaced men called up for the forces
had themselves been evacuated with their children as the V-1 and
V-2 threat increased. The *Nottingham Evening Post* reported
that in some pubs there had been outbreaks of 'panic drinking',
customers 'gulping their beer and shouting for an encore lest
their neighbours at the bar got more than they did'. At the same
time, in 'certain districts' only mild ale was available, because
bitter, which kept better, was earmarked for the troops. Many
pubs were only open for an hour and a half at lunchtimes and
two hours in the evening because they had no beer to sell, and
there was little relief even for those harvesting the grain that

A Spitfire IX fitted with the 'Mod XXX Depth Charge', modified bomb racks that could carry a cask of beer under each wing. (Vickers Armstrong publicity photograph)

would be used to make the new season's beers. In August 1944 it was announced that 'in some parts of Lincolnshire the beer famine has become so acute that many inns have announced that they will not be able to continue the age-old custom of supplying harvest beer this season. Cups of tea will be provided instead.'

4

The Bridal Gown – Echo of a Beery Celebration

It is surely a pleasing thought, as bride and bridegroom toast each other, that the 'bridal gown' she is wearing is named for a feast involving beer. 'Bridal', now an adjective, was originally a noun, 'bride-ale', in Anglo-Saxon *brýd-ealo*. The phrase meant 'wedding feast', with 'ale' being used here in its secondary sense of 'a festival or merry-meeting at which much ale was drunk' (just as 'tea' means both the drink and – as in 'afternoon tea' or 'high tea' – the meal). The same semantic extension is seen in the Irish expression for feasting, *coirm agus ceol*, which literally means 'ale and song' (well, what else does a celebration consist of?).

By the fourteenth century, 'bridal' had come to mean the whole proceedings of the wedding or marriage, not just the boozy meal after the ceremony, and it eventually became used, through misanalysis of the '-al' element, as the adjective for things to do with brides, such as in 'bridal gown'. But until Elizabethan times, or a little later, 'ale' could still mean 'festival' or 'celebration' as well as alcoholic drink, and 'bride-ale' still meant the whole wedding shebang. When Queen Elizabeth I visited Kenilworth Castle, the Warwickshire home of the Earl of Leicester, in July 1575, for example, among the entertainments put on for her – ranging from fireworks to feasting – was a 'country bryde ale' that included a bride and bridegroom picked from the local peasants, as well as the traditional wedding sport of 'running at the Quinting' or quintain, that is, tilting on horseback with lances at a pole set into the ground, and 'Morrice dancing'.

Detail from *The Wedding Feast* by Wenceslas Hollar (1607–77), after Bruegel. It is very likely the beer being drunk by the guests had been brewed by the bride and bridegroom. (University of Toronto)

Very probably, special brews would be made for those wedding feasts. A bride-ale could be expensive, and sometimes the bride or bridegroom brewed a wedding ale to sell to the guests to defray all or some of the costs of the party. With all the drinking, however, things could get out of hand, especially as wedding ales seem to have been strong ones; although one Elizabethan writer noted with satisfaction that there had been an improvement in his time in people's behaviour and 'the heathenish rioting at bride-ales are well diminished', with the authorities sometimes taking pre-emptive action. In 1572 the burgesses of the borough of Halesowen in the West Midlands declared,

A payne ys made that no person or persona that shall brewe any weddyn ale to sell shall not brewe above twelve stryke of mault [enough to make perhaps two barrels, 576 pints, of strong ale] at the most and that the said persons so marryed shall not keep nor have above eyght messe of persons at hys dinner within the burrowe [a 'messe' was four people, so that meant no more than 32 diners, giving an allowance of 18 pints a head!] and before hys brydall daye he shall keep no unlawfull games in hys house nor out of hys house on payne of 20s[hillings, or £1].

More light is shed on the brewing of ale for bride-ales or weddings by another ruling from the manorial court of Halesowen eight years later, which declared that no one should hold bride-ales unless they had been approved beforehand by the high bailiff and five other 'most substantial persons', and afterwards by the lord of the borough; that no one making a wedding ale should brew or sell the ale except on the day of the wedding and one day before and after; and that the ale should only be sold at the price charged by the victuallers of the borough (perhaps the local inn and alehouse owners were complaining about the competition), the fine for each offence being this time 40 shillings.

Today you will frequently see it claimed that the 'bride-ale' was the beer served at the feast, rather than the name of the feast itself. The man to blame for muddying the glass over the origin of the phrase 'bride-ale' is Thomas Dudley Fosbroke, Church of England priest and antiquarian, who claimed in a book called *Encyclopædia of Antiquities: and Elements of Archaeology, Classical and Mediæval*, published in 1825, that 'it was called Bride ale … from the bride's selling ale on the wedding day and friends contributing what they liked in payment.' Wrong, Mr Fosbroke. It was called '*A* bride-ale', not 'bride-ale', because 'an ale' was a general name for a feast. Such ales/feasts were often fundraisers, however, one of the most widespread being the 'church-ale', which was in existence by the start of the fifteenth century. This would be organised by the churchwardens, often at Whitsun, and the profit from the brewing and selling of drink, and the consumption of food to go with it, would be used for the maintenance of the local church, for paying for improvements such as a ring of bells or a new loft, or even for paying the parish clerk (in which case the festivities would be known as a 'clerk-ale').

Often the 'ale' was held in a building called the church-house. At least a couple of church-houses still survive in Devon, at South Tawton and Widecombe in the Moor. Frequently the 'ales' would be accompanied by plays, morris dancing, games and the like. They could raise considerable sums; in 1569 a church ale in another Devon village, Dean Prior, brought in £46 3s 4d, around £14,000 today. Other ales could be for non-ecclesiastical purposes. Lyme Regis in Dorset held regular 'cobb-ales' in the early seventeenth century to pay for keeping up the town's harbour; the one in 1601 raised £20 14s 10d. There were also lamb-ales, held after sheep-shearing had been completed, soul- or dirge-ales, held at funerals, and bid-ales, held to bring in funds for someone who had suffered an accident or was otherwise down on their luck.

The more Puritan-minded Tudor clergy were appalled by church-ales. In a sermon in 1570, a preacher named William *Kethe* claimed they were occasions for 'bul-beatings, beare-beatings, bowlings, dycing, cardyng, dauncynges, drunkenness and whoredom'. From this time, under pressure from Protestant clergy and local magistrates, church-ale celebrations began to disappear from many counties, particularly in the east and south-east of England, and to fall away in number elsewhere. Somerset seems to have been the last hold-out of the church-ale tradition, with the churchwardens in the coastal village of Williton still holding church-ales as late as the 1690s.

There are, incidentally, a number of ceremonies and traditions around weddings that involve beer and ale, including one called 'running for the bride's door'. In the Craven district in North Yorkshire, after the wedding ceremony had taken place at the church, according to a nineteenth-century writer, 'there took place either a foot or horse race, the first to arrive at the dwelling of the bride, requested to be shown to the chamber of the newly married pair; then, after he had turned down the bed-clothes, he returned, carrying in his hand a tankard of warm ale, previously prepared, to meet the bride, to whom he triumphantly offers the beverage.' The bride, in return for this, 'presented to the ale-bearer a ribbon as his reward'.

This is tame compared to what happened among the Turkic people of Chuvashia, on the banks of the Volga river in European Russia, some 400 miles east of Moscow. With the Chuvash, beer featured both before and after the wedding as a vital part of the ceremonies. Today, Chuvashia is Russia's hop-growing centre, and apparently it also has gypsum-bearing strata in its geology, just like the district around Burton upon Trent, Britain's great brewing town. Unsurprisingly then, Chuvashia is known in Russia for the quality of its beer. A visitor in the eighteenth century described how the bride, covered with a veil, hid herself behind a screen, from which after some time she went and walked round the eating room 'with a grave and solemn gait'. Some young girls 'bring her beer, honey and bread, and when she has gone three times round the room, the bridegroom enters, snatches off her veil, kisses her, and changes rings with her. From this instant she bears the name of *schourasnegher*, or betrothed girl, in quality of which she distributes bread, honey and beer to the guests, with which they refresh themselves.'

After the bride and bridegroom have retired to bed, the next day the guests come to check for confirmation that the bride was a virgin – 'the Mosaical proofs', as a writer in 1793 said, referring to Deuteronomy chapter 22, verses 15–17.

> If it appears that the bride had been deflowered before, a boy presents a mug filled with beer to one of the principal assistants. In the bottom of this mug is a hole, which the lad stops with his finger, but [he] draws it away when the other has the mug at his mouth, by which means the beer runs down his beard and bosom. This excites much laughter from the company and a blush from the bride. But this terrible ceremony is never followed by any more serious consequences.'

(The 'serious consequences' called for in Deuteronomy if the bride was not a virgin involved her being stoned to death. Happy times.)

Beer also featured in the marriage ceremony of the Chuvash people's near-neighbours further to the east, the Udmurts or Votjaks, a Finno-Ugric people who live in Udmurtia and who are said to be the most red-headed people in the world. An eighteenth-century visitor from England said that a pagan Udmurt wedding began with the bridegroom paying the *yerdoun*, or bride price, to his wife-to-be's father. The wedding guests then assembled in the bridegroom's father's house. The bride, having been clothed in the dress of a married woman, was presented to her new father-in-law. After this, while the *tor-kart* or priest made an offering of a cup of beer to the gods, the bride sat in the doorway upon a piece of cloth: the object of the offering was to grant bread, riches and children to the newly married couple, who drank the beer blessed by the priest. 'This done, one of the bridesmaids presents beer or mead to all the guests and the bride kneels down before every one of them till he has emptied his goblet: then they eat and drink as much as they are able, and dance till the young people are put to bed.'

The word 'bride' itself, incidentally, probably has beery connections too: it comes from a word that originally meant 'daughter-in-law' in the ancestor language of English, spoken in Jutland and Southern Sweden nearly 3,000 years ago, which looks to have come itself from a root word meaning 'to brew' and 'to cook, make broth' – the duties of a daughter-in-law in ancient times.

5

The British National Dinner – Roast Beef, Plum Pudding and Ale

Blame Charles Dickens. If he hadn't ended *A Christmas Carol* with the by-then thoroughly reformed Scrooge ordering the prize turkey to be delivered to the Cratchits' home in Camden, perhaps we would not now be persuaded in Britain that a tasteless, monstrous bird should be the centre of the Christmas dinner, and we would have stuck to the traditional yuletide treat – roast beef, lots of it, accompanied by plum pudding and strong ale.

If you search through nineteenth-century newspapers, it quickly becomes clear that the trinity of beef, heavy, dried-fruit-stuffed pudding and good ale was at the heart of the Christmas festivities everywhere in Britain, literally from palace to poorhouse. Here is the *Liverpool Weekly Mercury* for Saturday 29 September 1855.

THE ROYAL BARON OF BEEF

This old English joint was this year supplied to Windsor Castle by the royal purveyors at Windsor. The baron was cut from a five-year-old Highland Scot, fed by his Royal Highness Prince Albert, at the Norfolk Farm, and weighed 425lb. The process of roasting occupied 15 hours. It was decorated with holly and ivy, and placed cold on a sideboard in the banqueting-room on Christmas-day, where it will remain, together with the boar's head and woodcock pie, during the week.

It must have been pretty cold in that banqueting hall, for beef, pie and boar to remain healthy for a week. If you have not

John Bull in his glory; a Georgian print showing John Bull enjoying roast beef, plum pudding and ale. (Library of Congress British cartoon collection)

heard of a baron of beef, incidentally, Dr Johnson's dictionary says that 'a Baron of Beef is when the two sirloins are not cut asunder, but joined together by the end of the backbone' – in other words, an entire ox's backside.

At the same time as Victoria and the rest of the Saxe-Coburg-Gothas were cutting slices off 30 stone of cooked ox posterior, her poorest subjects were enjoying the same sort of treat. The Christmas Day workhouse meal of roast beef, plum pudding and ale had become an institution by the mid-nineteenth century; in London, on 25 December 1860, between 40,000 and 50,000 inmates of the metropolitan workhouses were supplied with roast beef and plum pudding. Even at the lower estimate, that is around 18 tons of beef, without bones, and perhaps 25 tons of pudding. Here is a tiny snatch of reports of the workhouse festivities around the country plucked from just one year, Christmas 1869, starting with the *Bristol Mercury* of Saturday 1 January 1870.

CHRISTMAS TREATS AT THE BRISTOL AND CLIFTON UNION WORKHOUSES

On Christmas-day the inmates at the Bristol Union at Stapleton and the Clifton Union at Fishpond-road were regaled with roast beef and plum pudding. The luxuries of beer, tobacco and snuff were added to the substantial Christmas fare; and the children were not forgotten on the festive occasion. At the Clifton Union there was a very imposing Christmas tree, loaded with books and toys to the value of about £8, for the youngsters ... Thanks to the efforts of the master and matron and their assistants, the interior of the building was very prettily decorated with evergreens, mottoes, and artificial flowers. No less than eight hundredweight of beef and eleven or twelve hundredweight of pudding were prepared for the Christmas feast; and in these days of complaints as to workhouse dietry and management, Clifton Union on Saturday last must have shown that even in the gloomy life of a pauper there are some gleams of sunshine.

The *Reading Mercury* for the same day, talking about events at Maidenhead, said,

CHRISTMAS AT COOKHAM UNION

On Christmas-eve each of the inmates in the men's and women's infirmaries enjoyed an extra cup of tea, ham, cakes &c., and just before bedtime each had a glass of mulled wine; this treat was given by the Master, Mr Malyon. In the evening the old men were regaled with a large mince pie and some of Nicholson's fine old ale, liberally given by Mr W. Nicholson, together with pipes and tobacco, all spending a pleasant evening with songs &c. On Christmas-day a substantial dinner, consisting of roast beef and plum pudding and ale, was given to each inmate.

That was William Nicholson, who had founded his brewery thirty years earlier in Maidenhead High Street; it finally closed in 1959, taken over by Courage & Barclay of London.

In the York Workhouse, the *York Herald* revealed,

> ... there were 480 inmates, exclusive of vagrants, on Christmas Day, which is the largest number of inmates ever present on a similar occasion ... By the kind liberality of the guardians and their friends this large number of paupers had the opportunity of partaking of the good old English fare with which the advent of Christmas is associated. A most substantial and first-class dinner was provided for them ... Upwards of 50 stones of prime roast beef, with mashed potato, comprised the first course, which was followed by 35 monster plum puddings, with brandy sauce, &c. The puddings consisted of 77 ½ lbs flour, 60lbs suet, 50lbs sugar, 60lbs currants, 14lbs raisins, 7lbs lemon peel, and 180 eggs. After dinner a suitable allowance of ale, tobacco &c. was made to the adults and fruits &c. distributed among the children.

Those puddings, to save you working it out, weighed around 8 lb each. They would have each been wrapped up in a cloth and hung, suspended, on a pole in a copper full of boiling water to cook – that copper being identical to the sort found in any small nineteenth-century brewery – with a coal fire underneath.

In Leighton Buzzard, Bedfordshire, according to the *Northampton Mercury*,

> The Workhouse on Christmas Eve was gaily decorated with various devices in holly, ivy, laurel, and winter flowers. At twelve o'clock on Christmas-day more than 100 old and young people sat down to a substantial dinner of roast beef, boiled round of beef, roast and boiled legs and shoulders of mutton, and a bountiful supply of plum pudding. Each adult male had also one pint of good home-brewed ale ... After supper each adult inmate had one pint of ale and one oz. of tobacco. The old women

had each one pint of ale, and snuff. The old people thoroughly enjoyed themselves, and repeatedly expressed their thanks to the guardians and ratepayers, also to the master and matron, who were indefatigable in their attention.

Not everybody had roast beef. The local newspaper in Winchester reported after Christmas Day 1859,

MILITARY CHRISTMAS
The soldiers in this garrison had their accustomed treat, viz, a plentiful supply of roast and baked pork (beef being no treat to them), plum pudding and good ale on Christmas day. We need hardly say that the gallant fellows thoroughly enjoyed their fare, and spent a most 'jolly' Christmas.

Truly, these soldiers were beefeaters.

Of course, the royal Christmas dinner, while based on the same principles as those given to the paupers, was distinctly grander; the official, printed menu for Christmas Day 1896 at Osborne House, Queen Victoria's home on the Isle of Wight, showed boar's head and woodcock pie on the sideboard with the roast baron of beef, just as it was forty-one years earlier, while the main board included turbot, roast turkey and chine of pork. Interestingly, the royal family ate their plum pudding with the 'relevé', the main part of the meal. Here are a couple of reports of workhouse Christmas dinners that suggest this happened elsewhere, too, starting with the *Essex Newsman* in Colchester, Saturday 29 December 1900, reporting on what it – correctly – called 'the last Christmas of the century' the previous Tuesday. Describing the celebrations at the local home for the mentally handicapped, the Eastern Counties' Asylum for Idiots and Imbeciles (*sic* – later the Royal Eastern Counties' Institution) at Essex Hall,

Letters, cards and parcels were delivered to each patient during the morning. At 12.30 all those who were well enough sat down to an excellent dinner of roast beef and plum pudding, followed by dessert.

A few years earlier the *Isle of Man Times*, on Tuesday 26

December 1893, wrote,

> On Christmas Day the inmates of the House of Industry were
> again the recipients of the usual good fare, which, at this season
> of the year, through the kindness of Mr HP Noble, JP, Villa
> Marina, they have for the last 25 years been privileged to enjoy
> ... At one o'clock over 50 of the inmates were served with the
> good old-fashioned Christmas dinner, consisting of roast beef,
> potatoes, plum pudding and the best ale. The dessert consisted
> of apples and oranges, to which were added tobacco and snuff.

And according to the *Liverpool Mercury*, when 1,330 sailors
and marines from the Channel Fleet were given dinner by the
mayor and citizens of Liverpool at St George's Hall in October
1888, the menu consisted of 'roast turkey and sausages, roast
goose with onions and apple sauce, roast beef, potatoes and
cauliflower, plum pudding, and apples and pears for dessert'.

That last, non-Christmassy reference to roast beef and plum
pudding is a pointer to the forgotten fact that, as one food
historian wrote, 'roast beef served with plum pudding is the
most evocative of past traditions of hospitality. It was once
Britain's prime celebration dish and a potent symbol of the
nation's character and cohesiveness.' Here's a report from the
Bury and Norwich Post of Wednesday 2 January 1805.

> On Christmas day, Lord Whitworth entertained the Holmesdale
> Volunteers, consisting of 700 men, at Seven Oaks in Kent, with
> a very hospitable dinner consisting of roast and boiled beef, and
> plum-puddings, with a quart of ale to each man and a half a
> crown for liquor. His Lordship gave 50l. to be distributed among
> the families of those who are labouring men.

The Holmesdale Volunteers were named for the Vale of
Holmesdale at the foot of the North Downs. Lord Whitworth
was a British diplomat whose wife, the former Duchess of
Dorset, brought into the marriage a good fortune and ownership
of Knole Park, Sevenoaks. Britain was back at war with France;

even as the Volunteers dined, Napoleon was preparing an invasion at Boulogne, within sight of the Kent coast. If his barges had sailed, the Volunteers would have been among the Britons attempting to stop him.

A few years later, though Britain was still fighting France, the nation united in celebration for the golden jubilee of George III in October 1810. The king and his family lived at Kew, in the grounds of what is now Kew Gardens, and Kew itself saw a substantial party on October 25.

The preparations for the celebration of this memorable day at Kew were completed yesterday. This morning was ushered in by the firing of cannon and the ringing of bells ... After divine service, about 100 persons were entertained with roasted beef and plum-pudding, set out on tables, within a spacious marquee, erected on Kew-Green, opposite the high road. Rounds of beef were likewise cut up for the benefit of the wives and children of such persons as are natives of Kew. Porter, ale, and punch were plentifully distributed. On the health of His Majesty being drank, fifty pieces of cannon were discharged.

Within four years, Napoleon had been defeated, and Britain, as the *Norfolk Chronicle* recorded on Saturday 14 May 1814, could celebrate again in the usual way.

CATTON FEAST; May 6
To celebrate the glorious success of England and her Allies, the Restoration of the Bourbons to France and the Termination of Hostilities in Europe, a liberal subscription was raised and expended in the following handsome manner:- Six tables, of 20 yards long each, were arranged in the form of a crescent, extending along the front of an elevated and ornamental grove opposite Mr Ives's lawn ... At two o'clock all the inhabitants who could attend, to the number of nearly 500, each wearing a white cockade, sat down to a plentiful supply of Old English fare, roast beef, plum-pudding, and strong ale; the plum-puddings supporting flags, on each of which was wrought some appropriate motto.

Of course, just ten months later Napoleon had escaped from exile on Elba, and Britain was back to war. The victory at Waterloo, however, meant more celebrations. Here's the *Hampshire Chronicle* of Monday 8 August 1814:

> On Saturday, at the Grainge Park, near Alresford, upwards of 300 of the poor of the adjoining parishes were bountifully regaled by Henry Drummond, Esq, in commemoration of the happy return of peace, with a good dinner, consisting of roast and boiled meat of every description, plum pudding and plenty of good old stingo ... Weyhill, on Tuesday the 2nd inst presented a scene truly gratifying for its novelty, taste and elegance. The bells of the parish were ringing, and a band of music playing at an early hour. The Farnham hops booths were decorated with laurel and other emblematic representations of old England's victories, crowned with a glorious peace. Tables were erected throughout the booths, which were amply supplied with beef, mutton, and plum pudding, where the worthy Rector, and most of the principal inhabitants, who were subscribers, dined together with 400 poor men, women and children, who were all regaled with good ale and strong beer, in which they drank the healths of the King, the Prince Regent and the naval and military heroes, with enthusiastic loyalty.

Weyhill, outside Andover, was one of the great agricultural fairs of England. It was a centre for the sale of all sorts of products, including hops from Farnham in Surrey, then a rival to Kent and Herefordshire for hop growing.

Why roast beef (and plum pudding and ale) stopped being the celebratory menu of Britain, I don't know. I don't really blame Dickens. Even in 1893, fifty years after *A Christmas Carol* was first published, the *Northern Echo*, talking about the Christmas preparations in Middlesbrough, could still say, 'The roast beef of old England is invariably associated with this season of the year ... Next to the Christmas beef the plum pudding secures the greatest amount of attention ...'

Quite likely, the disappearance of the roast beef of old

England from the Christmas menu was because, with increasing affluence, roast beef became – as it was for those Winchester soldiers in 1859 – 'no treat', but a weekly occurrence. Similarly, affluence brought wine, rather than beer, to the dining table. And, of course, we no longer have the servant class available to cook vast quantities of beef and boil huge numbers of plum puddings. The last reference I have been able to find to the 'traditional' celebration comes from the *Tamworth Herald* of Saturday 2 January 1932.

Poor Law Institution

The dining room and wards of Tamworth Poor Law Institution were pleasingly decorated. The service was taken by the Rev A. C. Smith. A large 'family' was catered for, numbering 170 inmates and 28 casuals. The usual Christmas fare was allowed by the Public Assistance Committee and included roast beef, roast pork, and vegetables, and plum pudding, tea and ale. Sweets, tobacco, cigarettes, fruits and nuts were distributed.

Today the plum pudding hangs on, hurrah, although yuletide is the only time of year it is seen now, and its name has changed to reflect this: Christmas pudding.

6

The Potboy in History, Literature and Art

I was born, in what Carl Jung (who believed in synchronicity and the like) would have insisted was no coincidence, on the site of an old pub, the Upper Flask in Hampstead, near the Heath. The pub closed in the second half of the eighteenth century, and the building that housed it was replaced in the early years of the twentieth by Queen Mary's Maternity Home. Today, it's nursing accommodation for the Royal Free Hospital, but over the decades tens of thousands of babies must have been born there. I wonder if we all like beer.

If you walk down Heath Street from the site of the Upper Flask towards Hampstead Tube Station you come to the side-road called The Mount. In 1852, the painter Ford Madox Brown, who was lodging in Heath Street, spotted a gang of workmen digging up the road here to lay drains and decided what a marvellous picture these heroes of labour would make. It took him eleven years to complete the painting, which he called, simply, *Work*. It is an allegorical masterpiece typical of the pre-Raphaelite period (though Madox Brown was not, strictly, a member of the pre-Raphaelites), where every character of the more than two-dozen portrayed, from the gentleman earning £15,000 a year to the effeminate flower seller, has a back-story. It's also still recognisably the same scene today, more than 160 years later, as you will see if you stand by the high brick wall on the left of the painting and look north – except the upper middle classes now go past in BMW X5s rather than on horseback.

Beer ho !   Be—e—er !

A Victorian potboy, carrying full, quart-sized, pewter
pots of beer and calling for customers, from *Old London
Taverns* by Edward Callow. (British Library)

Madox Brown wanted his painting to illustrate the nobility of
honest toil, but labour needs sustenance and refreshment, and
one of the navvies is draining a pewter pot of something uplifting
and alcoholic – porter, probably, given the era. In front of the
drinker, and shouting 'beer ho!' according to Madox Brown, who
wrote notes about all the people in the painting, is the fellow who
brought the navvy the beer, the potman from one of the nearby
pubs. He is fancily dressed in bowtie and waistcoat, and wearing
the apron of his calling; in his left hand he carries the potboy's

beer tray or pot-board, rather like a carpenter's wooden toolbox, which bore eight or ten beer pots and, on the top, clay pipes for those who wanted a smoke with their beer.

I like to think the potman was from the Holly Bush pub, barely a minute away round the corner and up Holly Bush Steps, my favourite Hampstead pub. It became licensed premises in the early nineteenth century, and preserves a more domestic layout of rooms off and behind the bar and down corridors, with wooden floors and high-backed settles. It also has on the wall a superb sign for the former Benskin's Cannon Brewery, Watford, dating from before 1895 (when Benskin's changed its trademark from a cannon to a pennant) and advertising Benskin's old and mild ales, pale ale and Imperial stout.

Unfortunately, Madox Brown's notes suggests his potman was from the larger, and classier, Coach and Horses or Nag's Head in Heath Street itself.

> The man with the beer-tray, calling 'beer ho!' so lustily, is a specimen of town pluck and energy contrasted with country thews and sinews. He is humpbacked, dwarfish, and in all matters of taste, vulgar as Birmingham can make him look in the nineteenth century [a reference to his gilt watch chain]. As a child he was probably starved, stunted with gin, and suffered to get run over. But energy has brought him through to be a prosperous beer-man, and 'very much respected,' and in his way he also is a sort of hero; that black eye was got probably doing the police of his master's establishment, in an encounter with some huge ruffian whom he has conquered in fight, and hurled through the swing-doors of the palace of gin prone on the pavement.

Madox Brown actually painted two copies of *Work*: one is in Manchester Art Gallery, and the other, slightly smaller version is normally in Birmingham Art Gallery. A few years ago, however, the Birmingham version was shown at the National Gallery in London as part of an exhibition called *Work, Rest and Play*, which brought together twenty-five pieces by artists as diverse as Canaletto, Gauguin and L. S. Lowry. A couple of other paintings in the exhibition had beery connections. One was *Skittle Players Outside an Inn* by the seventeenth-century Dutch artist Jan Steen, who was the son of a brewer, and a tavern-keeper himself, and painted a number of scenes inside and outside inns.

The other was *La Serveuse de Bocks* by Edouard Manet, portraying a waitress at the Brasserie de Reichshofen in Paris and created in 1878/9. Manet was apparently fascinated by the waitress's ability to hold several glasses of bock beer at once, and asked her to come and pose for him at his studio: waitresses serving at tables were a comparatively new phenomenon in Paris. The young woman agreed, but only if she could bring her boyfriend along to add some respectability – 'artist's model' was a synonym for 'prostitute'. Manet included the boyfriend in the picture; he's the 'customer' in the blue smock in the foreground, smoking a pipe just like the ones Madox Brown's potman was selling. *La Serveuse* comes in two versions as well. The other is in the Musée d'Orsay in Paris. For me, the National Gallery's Manet is the better. The waitress appears harassed and is looking to her left, out of the picture, doubtless at another customer who is trying to order some beer himself; in the Paris version she is looking straight at the viewer. It's also a much better picture, I think, than Manet's much more famous *Bar at the Folies Bergere*, with its depiction of a bottle of Bass pale ale amid the Champagne, which is static and dull by comparison.

Madox Brown painted *Work* at a time when the institution of the potman, and potboy, was about to give way before the rise of the barmaid and the waitress. A potboy appears in another iconic English work of art, William Hogarth's *Beer Street* of 1751, 101 years earlier – that's him at the door of the pawnbroker's on the right, passing through the pint that is all the impoverished 'uncle' (pawnbroker) in happy and contented Beer Street can afford, while everyone else is drinking quarts. As a word, 'potboy' is only a century or so older than that: the *Oxford English Dictionary* found its first use in an anonymous book published around 1662, titled *The Life and Death of Mrs. Mary Frith, Commonly Called Moll Cutpurse*. The potboy's cry of 'beer-ho' as he sought customers for a quick draught was one of the familiar sounds of London; a poem by the eighteenth-century writer Mary Darby Robinson called 'London's Summer Morning', written in 1775, says that amid 'the din of hackney-coaches, waggons, carts', 'the pot-boy yells discordant'.

History's most notorious potboy was Edward Oxford, an eighteen-year-old out-of-work barman who fired two pistols at the newly married (and pregnant) Queen Victoria as she and Prince Albert drove in a carriage up Constitution Hill from Buckingham Palace on 10 June 1840. Both shots missed. Oxford was arrested immediately at the scene, and put on trial at the Old Bailey for high treason less than a month later. However, he was acquitted on the grounds of insanity – the evidence for his madness included papers found at his lodgings setting out the rules of a (non-existent) secret society, called 'Young England', whose members were pledged to meet 'carrying swords and pistols and wearing crepe masks'. Oxford was ordered to be detained at the Bedlam hospital for the insane in Lambeth. Later, in 1864, he was transferred to the new Broadmoor Institution in Berkshire, before being released in 1867 on condition that he left the country. He went to Australia, where he is said to have earned his living as a house painter, dying, according to one source, in 1900.

Charles Dickens mentions potboys in several of his novels. The potboy's, or potman's, dual role as beer server and bouncer, indicated in the shiner worn by Madox Brown's potman, is alluded to by Dickens in *Our Mutual Friend* when he says that at the Six Jolly Fellowship Porters, ruled by the strict Miss Abbey, 'the white-aproned pot-boy with his shirt-sleeves arranged in a tight roll on each bare shoulder, was a mere hint of the possibility of physical force, thrown out as a matter of state and form'. Other jobs carried out by the potboy included taking down the shutters on the pub windows every morning and putting them back up at night, ensuring the spittoons were emptied and regulating the gas lights. Many probably had ambitions to run their own establishment, and some graduated to the post of landlord by marrying their former employer's widow.

The fullest recording of a potboy's work outside the walls of the pub was made by Alfred Rosling Bennett in a book called

Londoners in the Eighteen-Fifties and Sixties. Writing in 1924, Bennett (who was actually an electrical engineer rather than a social historian) contrasted the street scenes of his childhood with those of the mid-1920s.

Another member of our little world who has no counterpart in these later times was the perambulating potman. Public-houses in the 1850s were allowed to deliver liquor at customers' premises, and nearly every tavern did so, employing potmen for the purpose who carried wooden frames divided longitudinally into two compartments in which cans of ale, porter and stout were deposited, together with a measure or two; a parallel bar above affording the necessary carrying handle. On weekdays the supper hour was the principal time of activity for these potmen, but they appeared to better advantage on Sundays, when, as soon as the clock had struck one, they issued from their bars clad in spotless white aprons and, in warm weather, in equally immaculate shirt-sleeves, intent on serving the Londoner with his dinner beer. Staggering under the weight of a couple of frames they went the round of their customers, measuring what was required from the cans into gaping expectant jugs. I am not sure whether they were entitled to serve any pedestrian who wanted drink, but I think they could be called to a house by a chance customer.

But while the potboy was still filling orders for those wanting beer at home, or delivering porter for an aristocratic household's servants to drink with their meals, pubs, and potboys, were changing, and the potboy was already in decline. George Dodd, in *The Food of London*, published in 1856, wrote,

The Public-Houses of London ... have undergone great changes within the last few years. They have been transformed from dingy pot-houses into splendid gin-palaces, from painted deal to polished mahogany, from small crooked panes of glass to magnificent crystal sheets, from plain useful fittings to costly luxurious adornments. The old Boniface, with his red nose and his white apron, has made way for the smart damsels who

prepare at their toilettes to shine at the bar ... Even the pot- boy is
not the pot-boy of other days; there is a dash of something about
him that may almost be called gentility; his apron is cleaner than
were the aprons of pot-boys twenty years ago; and the tray filled
with quarts and pints of dinner-beer, carried out to the houses of
the customers, seems to have undergone some change, for it is less
frequently seen than 'in days of yore'.

John Camden Hotten's *Slang Dictionary* of 1874 says the
'backslang' for a potboy was 'top-yob', which is a clue to the
job's social standing: 'from potboy to peer' was a phrase *The
Times* used in the nineteenth century to indicate the widest
possible range of society. The *Daily Telegrap*h journalist James
Greenwood, who specialised in low-life exposés, recorded in a
book called *The Wilds of London* – published the same year
as Hotton's slang directory – being confused by backslang in a
flyer for a 'rat-killing' event for members of the 'Canine fancy' to
be held at Billy Skunko's Turnspit pub, Quaker's Alley, Somers
Town, in the East End of London: 'Rats in the pit at Half-past
Eight precisely. Previous to the above entertainment, Mr Chitley
will sing his finch Peeler against Edward the Topyob's celebrated
bird, for a pound a side.' Edward was presumably an employee,
as potboy, of Mr Skunko at the Turnspit: competitive finch-
singing is still practiced in Flanders.

'Pot-boy-dom' was a tough job: the Victorian writer George
Gissing (admittedly English literature's greatest miserabilist),
in his novel *The Nether World*, set around 1880, described
the life of eighteen-year-old Stephen Candy. 'Stephen pursued
the occupation of a potman; his hours were from eight in the
morning till midnight on week-days, and on Sunday the time
during which a public-house is permitted to be open; once a
month he was allowed freedom after six o'clock.'

However, several developments were conspiring to eradicate
the potboy. The passing of the 'grocer's licence' Act in 1860,
allowing shops to retail wines and beers for consumption off the
premises – 'off-licences' – meant pubs no longer had an effective
monopoly on the 'carry-out' trade. The increasing popularity of

bottled beers meant households could stock up with drink rather than having to send out as required for the potboy to make a 'just-in-time' delivery. Finally, young working-class women were seeing serving in bars as a respectable alternative to working as a servant in the homes of the middle and upper classes – and pub owners were starting to prefer barmaids as well. The Reverend Charles Maurice Davies wrote in 1875 in *Mystic London*,

> The discriminating visitor will decidedly prefer to receive his sandwich and glass of bitter at the hands of a pretty barmaid rather than from an oleaginous potman in his shirt-sleeves; and the sherry-cobbler acquires a racier flavour from the arch looks of the Hebe who dispenses it. If silly young men do dawdle at the bar for the sake of the sirens inside, and occasionally, as we have known to be the case, take unto themselves these same sirens 'for better or for worse,' we can only cite the opinion of well-informed authorities, that very possibly the young gentlemen in question might have gone farther and fared worse, and that it is not always the young lady who has, in such a case, the best of the bargain.

By the time of the First World War, when, in any case, fit young men not in reserved occupations would be called up to fight the Kaiser rather than working in pubs, the potboy was effectively extinct. The expression potboy lingered in the twentieth century only as a lightly contemptuous term for the elderly pensioner every 'local' used to have, who, generally for the price of a pint of mild, would act as semi-unofficial collector-up of used glasses at the end of every session. It was a long fall from Madox Brown's 'prosperous beer-man' of the 1850s.

7

Dutch Schultz, Beer Hero?

Dutch Schultz insisted right up to his violent death at the age of thirty-three that he never did anything to deserve the 'nation's top gangster' label that J. Edgar Hoover and the FBI stuck on him. All he did, he said, was 'supply good beer to people who wanted it. And a lot of them did.'

Unfortunately, supplying beer was illegal. The Eighteenth Amendment to the Constitution had imposed Prohibition on the whole United States from 1 January 1920, and the sale of any sort of alcohol was banned. Besides, Schultz was involved in shady areas of enterprise other than brewing: there were the protection rackets, the illegal lotteries, the feuds with rival bootleggers and the bribing of politicians and police officers. But for a gangster, Dutch Schultz was a moral man. As he told a newspaper reporter in 1929, 'I may do a lot of lousy things, but I'll never make a living off women or narcotics.'

This was someone, however, who had personally shot dead at least two of his own men that he suspected of taking more money than was their due. His dealings with rivals were no less drastic. Even as prohibition was ending, in 1933, Schultz settled a row with another beer baron, Max Hassel, by having him gunned down in a hotel suite in New Jersey. When Schultz was killed himself, by fellow gangsters, he was threatening to assassinate the New York special prosecutor, Thomas Dewey.

Dutch Shultz was not, in fact, Dutch, and nor was his name Schultz. He was born Arthur Flegenheimer in the Bronx, New York, in 1902, son of German-Jewish immigrants. Arthur quit school at twelve and tried various jobs before deciding that burglary was easier, and brought in more money.

Unfortunately, in January 1919, aged sixteen, he was arrested coming out of an apartment in the upper Bronx with items that did not belong to him. A term in jail followed, where he hit a guard and escaped for all of fifteen hours. He returned to the Bronx after a total of a year and a quarter inside – the only prison sentence he ever served. His fellows in the local street gang, who had heard about the knockabout with the guard, nicknamed him Dutch Schultz after a fighter from the past.

For a while, Arthur 'Dutch Schultz' Flegenheimer was working in a small way for Jack 'Legs' Diamond, who was running a little speakeasy in the Bronx. Then Arthur started working for a local trucking business that, since the arrival of Prohibition, specialised in the now-illegal vocation of delivering beer. It was his job to ride shotgun on the beer trucks, protecting them from hijack by rival bootleggers.

The role enabled the young man to get a picture of the economics involved in making and selling beer in legally 'dry' New York. A limited number of breweries were still operating, with licences to produce 'near beer', containing 0.5 per cent or less of alcohol (this gave them an excuse for the smell of hops and mashing malt around their premises). Some also produced real beer on the sly, behind locked doors, for sale to the speakeasies that had burst into existence once drinking was forced underground. At others, the casks of near-beer they made legally were spiked with alcohol knocked out in a backroom still (much easier to hide than a brewery) to make 'needle beer', so-called after the syringes used to inject the extra alcohol into the casks through the bungholes, strong as the pre-Prohibition stuff.

The near-beer was brewed for just $3 or $4 a barrel. It cost less than 50 cents to buy enough alcohol to turn that barrel into needle beer. The distributors bought the needle beer for $8 or $9, and sold it to the speakeasies and tavern keepers for $18 or $19. They in turn sold it on to their thirsty customers for the equivalent of twice as much again. Everybody made a profit along the way. But a man did not need a degree in economics to see that someone who controlled the entire chain, from brewery to bar – what is known in business as 'vertical integration' – could keep the whole proceeds. Dutch could see there were a lot of proceeds to be gathered from selling beer at 15 cents a glass that had been made for only 15 cents a gallon.

Young Arthur – he was still just twenty-six – shifted from being a small cog in the distribution machine to a partnership with a friend called Joey Noe (pronounced noy) in a tenement speakeasy in the Bronx. The business was a success, and the two opened further outlets. Then they moved into the beer delivery business themselves, to supply their own bars, buying their product from a brewery in Union City, New Jersey. The next step was to supply other speakeasies in the district with beer. The owners of rival outlets were generally easily persuaded that it would be better for their health to buy beer from the Schultz/ Noe partnership, though one, an Irishman called Joe Rock, tried to resist. He was kidnapped, beaten, hung by his thumbs from a meat hook and blinded; he was sent home only after his family had paid a ransom of $35,000.

The pair began to expand their operation outside the Bronx, into other areas of New York, such as Washington Heights and Harlem. They were selling so much beer they had to go to other producers for supplies, including the Phoenix brewery on Tenth Avenue and 26th Street in New York. This was controlled by Owney Madden, an English-born gangster (either Liverpool or Leeds, depending on which source you trust) of Irish ancestry who owned the Cotton Club in Harlem, where black dancers and jazz bands entertained white customers, and whose 'Madden's No. 1' was Manhattan's favourite brew. (Madden was played by the actor Bob Hoskins in the film *Cotton Club*, though in truth he looked nothing like Hoskins.)

However, rival beer suppliers resented Schultz and Noe's arrival in their territory – one such being 'Legs' Diamond, who had already been pushed out of the Bronx beer business by the newcomers. In October 1928, Joey Noe was shot and mortally wounded outside a nightclub on West 54th Street, near 6th Avenue, by gunmen in the employ of Diamond, though not before he had fired enough bullets back to kill one of his assassins. When Legs Diamond himself was killed three years later in a boarding house in Albany, it was generally agreed that Dutch Schultz had arranged the deed in revenge for his friend and partner.

Meanwhile the Dutchman had acquired a controlling interest in a brewery in Chicken Island, Yonkers, being run as the State Cereal Beverage Co. Accounts differ on how Schultz obtained control, although it seems likely it involved the sort of offer that persuaded bar owners to agree to take his beer. At last he owned the whole beer chain, from manufacturing to retail sale. Even a bloody eighteen-month war with a rival gangster, Vincent 'Mad Dog' Coll – which finally ended with Coll being Tommy-gunned in a drugstore phone booth – failed to stop the dollars flooding through from the booze business. The federal authorities were to claim that Schultz's personal income from his illegal bootlegging activities, for the three years from 1929 to 1931, amounted to $481,637.35 of taxable earnings. It was a multimillion-dollar business being run by a man not yet in his thirties.

Schultz was powerful enough by the late 1920s to be invited to join the meetings organised by his fellow New York gangster Lucky Luciano to set up a national crime syndicate. He had also moved in on an even more lucrative operation than bootlegging, the illegal lotteries known as the numbers game or policy racket. Most of the sums staked on the numbers game by punters were tiny. But so many people – generally poor – played that they amounted, by the time Schultz and his heavies took almost complete control of New York operations, to an income of $20 million a year. Much of this had to be paid back in bribes to New York's politicians and policemen, but Schultz was still easily a very rich man. Not that anyone could tell from looking; he was notoriously poorly dressed, believing it a waste of money to spend on clothes.

In 1933 Franklin Roosevelt took office as President of the United States. As a preliminary to the eventual ending of Prohibition, Roosevelt declared that 3.2 per cent beer would no longer be regarded as intoxicating, and was now legal.

Dutch Shultz could be a legitimate brewer. He bought Owney Madden's brewery, and another in Brooklyn. He could not quite get to grips with the new business climate, however. When a rival brewer began selling barrels in the Bronx, Schultz had his opponent's delivery truck hijacked, and had to be told by his political contacts that, with beer now legal, this was no longer an acceptable tactic.

Schultz had bigger worries than rival brewers, though. A federal grand jury had just returned an indictment against him on eleven counts of income tax evasion, totalling more than $92,000. He immediately went into hiding while his lawyer pulled strings to get the case heard away from the city and in upstate New York, where the jury might be more friendly. It was at this point that Hoover and the FBI put Schultz's face in Post Offices around the United States in an attempt to find the fugitive, now officially 'Public Enemy Number One'. Schultz finally turned up for his trial in the autumn of 1934, only to have to face a retrial after the jury failed to agree. At the second hearing, however, the new jury returned a finding of not guilty – to the amazement and fury of the presiding judge.

Schultz was not out of trouble yet. Tom Dewey (who went on to be Governor of New York and the losing Republican candidate for President of the United States in 1944 and 1948) was investigating the numbers game, and also the protection racket the Dutchman had begun operating among New York's restaurants and cafes in 1932. In October 1935, at a meeting in Manhattan, Schultz urged Luciano and the other big crime bosses to arrange for Dewey to be killed. When they demurred, Schultz announced that he would organise it himself and left the meeting.

Once he had gone, the others agreed – Schultz himself was now a dangerous menace, because of the wrath he could bring down on them all if he went after Dewey. Never kill newspapermen, politicians or prosecutors, the Mob agreed. Too much trouble would follow. The Dutchman had to die.

A few days later, two hit men walked into the Palace Chop House, Newark, where Schultz was holding a meeting with three gang members. The bullets flew, leaving Schultz and his three henchmen mortally wounded, in the worst gangland slaying since the St Valentine's Day massacre in Chicago in 1929.

The Dutchman, bringer of beer to the people of New York, was struck by a single bullet that ripped through him, causing irreparable damage. He died twenty-four hours later in Newark City Hospital, surrounded by policemen trying unsuccessfully to get him to say who his assailants had been. The Beer Baron of the Bronx was gone, dead as the Prohibition legislation that brought him into being.

8

The True Story Behind Britain's Most Popular Pub Name

The Red Lion is often claimed to be the commonest pub name in Britain (though at around 650 examples it is probably just beaten by the Crown). However, despite its popularity (or perhaps because of it), there is an amazing amount of nonsense talked about why so many pubs are called the Red Lion.

One common claim is that most Red Lion pubs have their origins in the reign of James I. The story alleges that the new king, who had already been king in Scotland for some time, ordered that all the buildings of public importance display the red lion of Scotland as a sign of their allegiance to him; this included all of the inns and taverns.

Let's just forensically dissect this claim. First, is there any evidence at all that James VI/I made such an order?

No.

Second, would there be a sensible motive for him to make such an order?

No, quite the opposite. James had been the heir presumptive to Queen Elizabeth since the death of his mother, Mary Queen of Scots, in 1587, but it had never been certain he would be offered the crown; although he arrived in London with a fair degree of goodwill from the bulk of the English population, he would not have pushed the fact that they were now ruled by a king from another country in their faces by insisting that Scottish red lions be put up everywhere.

Third, if such an order had been made, is it likely it would have affected pub and inn names?

The Red Lion, Fulwell – West London – nothing to do with John of Gaunt, or King James I. (Author's collection)

No – if all the 'buildings of public importance' bore red lions on them (and incidentally, the claim begs the question that a tavern would be seen as a 'building of public importance' anyway, a highly dubious assumption), then how could you tell, if someone said, 'I'll meet you at the Red Lion,' which 'Red Lion' was which?

So, to sum up on the claim that the Red Lion pub name comes from a decree by James I in 1603, there's no evidence for it, it doesn't make sense historically and it's nonsense from a practical direction as well.

Perhaps the most common explanation for the origins of the pub name Red Lion is that it is derived from the badge of John of Gaunt, who died in 1399. This is the origin you will find in almost every book on pub names, including Jacob Larwood and John Camden Hotten's *The History of Signboards*, first published in 1866, which declares that 'doubtless' John of Gaunt's red lion spawned all the other Red Lions. But it doesn't take much research to show that this, too, is nonsense.

A red lion was certainly one of the badges linked to John of Gaunt, Edward III's fourth son, who was born in the city now spelt Ghent in Flanders. He was Duke of Lancaster (through his first wife, Blanche) and also a claimant to the throne of the kingdoms of Castile and Leon in Spain through his second wife, Constance of Castile. Leon's arms, naturally, were a (usually red – though some sources say purple) lion rampant on a silver background, and during the time John laid claim to the throne of Leon he must have used those arms.

John was one of the most powerful men in later fourteenth-century Britain; he was Steward of England from the time the young Richard II came to the throne and the richest man in the country, with an income of £12,000 a year. He was, effectively, founder of the House of Lancaster, being father, grandfather and great-grandfather to Henrys IV, V and VI respectively, and, through his third marriage, great-great grandfather of Henry VII, first of the Tudors. All subsequent British monarchs are his descendants. He is thus a very important English historical figure.

However, he was haughty and reserved and was deeply disliked during his life among the bulk of English people for his policies towards the oppressed masses. In the Peasants' Revolt of 1381, when he was out of the country, the rebels destroyed his palace by the Thames in London, the Savoy. Rather than loot the palace, the attackers threw the duke's gold and silver onto a bonfire and his jewels into the Thames. They said they refused to steal from such a hated figure. One man who did try to pillage was also thrown on the fire. When John did return to England he was largely responsible for crushing the rebellion. It is unimaginable that such an unpopular man should have had his badge on so many pubs.

In addition, John only had the right to the red lion of Leon for the seventeen years between 1371, when he married Constance, and 1388, when he gave up his claim to the Spanish thrones in return for £100,000 (an unbelievably large sum of money in the fourteenth century – equal to perhaps £2.5 billion today) and a yearly pension.

So, not John of Gaunt either, then. Who else? Well, the red lion is, in fact, one of the commonest heraldic badges in England. More than 150 families, in at least thirty-one counties from Cornwall to Northumberland, bore the 'lion gules' (including at least one family of brewers, the Stewards of Norfolk). With the red lion in such widespread use by those entitled to bear arms, who were almost by definition important landowners – and frequently lords of the manor – in the places where they lived, it is not surprising that the common use of the red lion among the English aristocracy and gentry is reflected in our pub signs. In the village of Chenies, Buckinghamshire, for example, the big local landowner and lord of the manor was the Duke of Bedford, whose Russell family arms showed a red lion. The village's two pubs are still called the Bedford Arms and – yes – the Red Lion.

A heraldically derived pub name need not even be from a family with property interests in the immediate vicinity. Sometimes noble visitors took their personal signs with them on their travels, to put up on houses where they and their supporters were lodging. These signs, bearing the family badge and intended to show the illiterate where the lord's retinue could be found in a strange town, were known as 'lodging escutcheons'.

In 1560 the then Earl of Bedford, ancestor to the later Dukes, took with him 'iij dozen of logyng skochyons' (lodging escutcheons) on a journey to France. Undoubtedly his 'logyng skochyon' was the Russell red lion, and if he and his retinue stayed in the same inns regularly, many of those inns must have gained permission to display a red lion permanently to show their connection with this noble family. There was a Red Lion in Bedford itself, and it is recorded that in 1689 the fifth Earl of Bedford stayed in state at the Red Lion, Cambridge – surely not a coincidence. On his way there he stopped for a night in Royston, Hertfordshire – where one of the biggest inns was, again, the Red Lion.

The truth is that there is no single, easy answer to the origin of the Red Lion, such as 'James I', or 'John of Gaunt', but a multitude of answers, each one particular to a specific place. Each pub will have been called the Red Lion for its own reason, generally connected to specifically local concerns. The Red Lion, Cambridge, will have a different origin for its name to the Red Lion, Cerne Abbas, or the Red Lion, Osset, West Yorkshire, and only local research can tease out the likely true story for each different Red Lion pub.

9

When the Stately Homes of England Drank Twenty-One-Year-Old Ale

In November 1898 an heir was born to the sixth Earl of Caernarvon, and at Highclere Castle, the earl's Hampshire home (and the place where the television series *Downton Abbey* is filmed), preparations were begun for the continuation of an important and ancient tradition. This tradition was the brewing of vast quantities of ale, to be laid down for twenty-one years and drunk when the newlyborn Lord Porchester reached the age of majority. A cask capable of holding 4,000 pints of ale, made from well-seasoned oak grown on the Highclere estate, was commissioned from Sam Walter, a Newbury cooper. The finished cask, banded with massive brass hoops, bore a brass coronet and an inscription plate that said, 'May Highclere Flourish. This cask of ale, containing 500 gallons, was brewed in commemoration of Lord Porchester, born November 7th, 1898. Albert Streatfield, butler, Highclere Castle 1898.' The ale itself was brewed in March 1899 (March and October were the traditional months for brewing strong drink) and tapped at Lord Porchester's coming-of-age party at Highclere in November 1919.

Sadly, the Highclere coming-of-age ale was one of the last examples of massively aged aristocratic ale; few stately homes still had their own estate breweries, though they had once been almost universal. Great houses such as Highclere had certainly brewed their own ale and beer for centuries, to supply the family and their servants and estate workers – probably most farmers in Britain, in fact, had domestic breweries up to the middle or so

A satirical print by Isaac Cruikshank (*c.* 1764–1811), published after the Duke of Rutland's twenty-first birthday celebrations in 1799, suggesting some of the scenes at Belvoir Castle as the guests arose the next day. (Library of Congress British cartoon collection)

of the nineteenth century. But by 1899, very few families could afford to pay the tax on several hundred gallons of ale and then let it slumber in cellars for more than two decades.

The coming-of-age ale looks to have developed in the early eighteenth century, as private brewers began to keep their strong ales longer and longer before drinking them. In 1703, the *Guide to Gentlemen and Farmers for Brewing the Finest Malt Liquors* declared that 'many country gentlemen … talk of, and magnify their stale Beer of 5, 10 or more years old' ('stale', here, meaning mature, and not 'off'). For a hogshead (54 gallons) of strong March or October ale, the *Guide* suggested using 11 bushels of malt, which would have given an original gravity in the 1130s or 1140s and a strength of perhaps 11 or 12 per cent alcohol by volume, or more.

One of the earliest coming-of-age ales recorded was laid down in 1730, at Wentworth House in Yorkshire, on the birth of

Charles Watson-Wentworth, son of Thomas Watson-Wentworth, who became the first Marquess of Rockingham in 1846. Thomas died in 1750, making Charles the second Marquess, and when Charles came of age the following May, a huge celebration was held at Wentworth House with 'upwards of 10,000 guests' in total, of whom 3,000 were entertained in the house. The food provided included 110 dishes of roast beef, seventy pies, sixty-six dishes of mutton, forty-eight hams, fifty-five dishes of lamb, seventy dishes of veal, forty dishes of chicken and 104 dishes of fish, while the drink included thirteen hogsheads of ale, twenty hogsheads of strong beer (beer and ale were still separate at this time, with the ale normally less hoppy but stronger), eight hogsheads of punch and four hogsheads of wine. The strong beer was 'most of it brew'd in the Year 1730', the *Derby Mercury* reported, adding that the whole affair 'was conducted with as great Regularity as could be expected where there was so great a Concourse of people'.

The earliest eyewitness (or tongue-witness) account of extreme-aged cask ale comes from the actor-manager John Bernard, who wrote in 1830 about a visit he made in around 1793/4 to Mount Edgcumbe House, home of the Earl of Mount Edgcumbe, close by Plymouth Sound in what is now Cornwall but was then Devon. The earl pressed Bernard and his companions

> to taste the family ale, for which Mount Edgecombe [*sic*] enjoyed some celebrity. It had been brewed on the birth day of Lord Valletort [the earl's eldest son, born 13 September 1764] , and was not broached till he came of age [i.e. in 1785]: it was more mild than the eulogised liquor of Boniface, but equally potent. Jefferson incautiously smacking his lips after emptying his glass induced his Lordship to fill it again, and this being a precedent not to be overruled in regard to ourselves, we all found it a difficult matter to pursue our path to the tavern with that due preservation of the perpendicular which people usually maintain before dinner.

Bernard and his friends were drinking ale that was at least twenty-nine years old and had been first tapped at least eight years earlier. The tradition was kept up at Mount Edgcumbe

House for at least three more generations: when the great-grandson of Bernard's Viscount Valletort came of age in August 1886, the *Hampshire Advertiser* recorded, 'At the dinner to the tenantry, ale was drunk which was brewed in October twenty-one years ago [in 1865], in celebration of Lord Valletort's birth. This ale had been kept in a two-hundred-gallon cask, and refreshed every seven years with new hops.' Adding fresh hops every seven years was, presumably, a trick the staff at Mount Edgcumbe House had learnt between 1785 and 1865 to keep super-aged ale in form. Another trick was topping up the cask of ale, on the solera system. An article written in 1899 asserted that it was still 'a common thing in England to make a large brew of beer when the heir to an estate is born. This is stored in casks, the loss by evaporation being supplied, from time to time, by adding fresh beer. When the heir reaches his majority, the beer is dispensed to the guests at the coming of age rejoicings.'

Another coming-of-age ale was brewed in 1764 at the birth of John Dawnay, eldest son of the fifth Viscount Downe, whose home was Cowick Hall in East Yorkshire. John had become Lord Downe himself by 1785 when his twenty-first birthday was celebrated at Cowick Hall by a mere 500 people, who dined on a large ox, 'several sheep, calves, hams, turkies, geese, many sorts of other fowle with game', and 'extremely good' twenty-one-year-old strong beer, according to the *Derby Mercury*.

At Belvoir Castle (pronounced 'beever') in Leicestershire, home of the Manners family, Dukes of Rutland, on 4 January 1799 several hundred 'persons of the first rank', including the Prince of Wales, were entertained with a dinner and ball to celebrate the young duke's coming of age, with 'the whole inhabitants of 10 neighbouring parishes' invited along for their own entertainments, making, according to one estimate, 10,000 other guests in the castle grounds. The entire affair was estimated to cost £10,000 (perhaps £10 million today), including £500 on lighting. Among the attractions – for the nobility, at least – were sixty pineapples at 2 guineas each (more than £150 today), while for the tenantry there was 'roast beef, porter and strong beer, brewed at the birth of this young nobleman', that is, in 1778.

From the start of the nineteenth century, references to coming-of-age ale being drunk begin to crop up, if not regularly, at least often enough to show that such brews were not totally unusual. When an eldest son was born to the Earl of Berkeley (the man who gave his name to the Berkeley Hunt of cockney rhyming slang notoriety) in December 1786, for example, a cask containing four hogsheads of special brew was filled at the family seat, Berkeley Castle, Gloucestershire, and tapped twenty-one years later, in 1807, at a celebration in the Great Hall at the castle. The party was attended by the Duke of Clarence (later William IV), among many others, and as well as the aged ale it featured a twenty-one-gun salute fired from the castle walls, 5,000 coloured lamps and, if the ale was not enough, 'two immense bowls of Punch, each containing twenty gallons'.

Similarly, when a son and heir, the magnificently monikered Richard Plantagenet Temple Nugent Brydges Chandos Grenville, Viscount Temple, was born to the Marquess of Buckingham at Stowe House in February 1797, vast casks in the cellars were again filled with ale in anticipation of his coming of age twenty-one years later. Thomas Frognall Dibdin, who saw the 'monstrous' casks in 1815 or 1816, two years or so before they were broached at a celebration attended by 'a great concourse of the first nobility', described them as 'a regiment of barrels only exceeded in grenadier height by those which I saw at Heidelberg in 1818.'

The minor gentry were also laying down ales intended for super-ageing. When Sir John Davie, of Creedy House, near Crediton, Devon, turned twenty-one in March 1817, 'three fat oxen and 15 hundred shilling loaves were distributed to the poor. All the tenantry were hospitably entertained at the mansion and hogsheads of ale born on the birth-day of the Baronet were tapped, for the first time, in honour of the day.'

One of the biggest celebrations took place in September 1841, when the 'magnificent mansion' of Wynnstay, near Wrexham in North Wales, saw four days of celebration to mark the coming of age of Sir Watkin Williams-Wynn. On the last day, 500 people, including Sir Watkin's uncles the Duke of Northumberland and the Earl of Powis, sat down to dine in a 7,500-square-feet pavilion, 20 feet high, erected in the garden. The menu included rounds and sirloins of beef, shoulders and legs of lamb, haunches of venison, roast and boiled chickens, grouse, partridges, jugged hare, veal, hams, salmon, carp, tench, lobster salad, tongues, jellies, blancmanges and pastries, 'unlimited' wines including claret, hock, champagne and port – and 'probably the greatest treat', according to the local newspaper, the *Shropshire Conservative*, 'an abundant supply of rare old ale, brewed at the birth of the present Sir Watkin Wynn', that is, twenty-one years earlier, in 1820, 'when 200 bushels of malt were brewed to fill the noble barrel out of which the company were supplied with their invigorating potations'. Sir Watkin, the sixth baronet, and his cellarer, Mr Martin, who had been at Wynnstay for nearly half a century, drank the first jug of twenty-one-year-old ale between them, and were evidently quickly joined by the duke and earl. 'Those highest in rank in the company appeared to enjoy the noble liquor with the utmost relish,' the *Shropshire Conservative* said.

In February 1845, the celebrations for the coming of age of the Marquess of Worcester, eldest son of the Duke of Beaufort, which took place at the assembly rooms in Swansea, included a song requesting that 'in each happy heart this day may memory keep alive, when with Old Ale brewed in '24 we drank in '45!'

It was not just rural areas that enjoyed coming-of-age beer. At the twenty-first birthday in January 1850 of the Honorable Augustus Henry Venables-Vernon, son of the fifth Baron Vernon, owner of the coal mines at Poynton in Cheshire, 1,500 miners employed by Lord Vernon sat down in Poynton School to a dinner of beef from two 'immense' oxen and 'liberal potions of prime old stingo ale, brewed in 1829, at the birth of the present heir of Poynton'.

Nor was it necessary (although it helped) to be heir to a title to enjoy extreme-aged ale at your twenty-first birthday party. The coming-of-age of Lieutenant Philip Bennet of the Royal Horseguards in December 1858 – the eleventh Philip

Bennet in succession, and son of the local MP – at Rougham
Hall, near Bury St Edmonds in Suffolk, saw a dinner for fifty
and a ball for 300 of the local 'nobility and gentry', while
'connoisseurs in malt liquor had an opportunity of tasting some
extraordinary ale, brewed at the birth of the young heir, the
strength of which, according to general report, rivalled that of
the wonderful beverage whose appalling potency in causing the
premature demise of Mr Topsawyer, as related by the "friendly
waiter", excited so much alarm in the breast of poor little David
Copperfield'.

Sometimes, it appears, it was a servant who nudged the
father into brewing. During the coming-of-age celebrations of
Charles Mainwaring, son and heir of another MP, Townshend
Mainwaring of Galltfaenan in Denbighshire, North Wales, in
July 1866, Mr Mainwaring senior announced that 'a good old
servant' had come to him at the birth of his son in 1845 and said
that 'if the child was spared he would one day come of age, and
they had better brew a barrel of ale for the occasion. That ale
was brewed, and had that day been tapped, and he hoped they
would taste it.'

Records of coming-of-age ales from the south-east of England
appear to be rare, though in August 1872 the twenty-first
birthday celebrations of Lord Clifton, eldest son of the Earl of
Darnley, at Cobham Hall, near Rochester, Kent, saw what was
called 'the usual large vat of ale, brewed at the birth of the heir
to the earldom ... tapped, and the health of his lordship heartily
drunk.' Cobham Hall had several large oast houses in the
grounds, and it seems certain Lord Clifton's twenty-one-year-old
ale would have contained Kentish hops.

Sir Henry Monson de la Poer Beresford-Peirse and his bride,
the Lady Adelaide, returned from their Continental wedding
tour early in 1874 to their home, Bedale Hall in North
Yorkshire, and in June a grand festival was held to mark Sir
Henry's formal installation as landlord of the Bedale Estates. At
the dinner were two casks that had been filled with 100 gallons
of 'prime ale' when Sir Henry was born in September 1850, and
which had remained in the cellars at Bedale Hall since then.

The *York Herald* remarked that 'the mouldy appearance of the exterior' of the casks 'sufficed to show their "antiquity", and to connoisseurs the quality of the "nut-brown" ale within, which was afterwards handed round the table, and enjoyed in all its pungency'.

In 1873, Lady Blanche Noel, daughter of the Earl of Gainsborough, wrote about the twenty-first birthday celebrations of her eldest brother, Charles, Viscount Campden, two years earlier at the family home, Exton Hall, Rutland. 'The universal custom in England of brewing a large quantity of the very best ale the year an heir is born and keeping it untouched until the day he becomes of age, when the cask is broached and distributed in prudently moderate quantities to the guests and tenants, is of very ancient origin and is most religiously adhered to,' she said. On the day of Lord Campden's birthday, 'Directly after breakfast we went up to the old hall to see the gigantic cask of twenty one years' old ale opened and, as in duty bound, to taste the ale to Charles's health ... The cavernous cellar in which stand the mysterious casks, the ivy-grown ruin overhead, the brawny men opening the family treasures and serving as rustic cup bearers to the guests, all made a thorough old-time picture.'

Later in the day Lord Campden and his family shared the birthday dinner with, again, 500 guests, the menu this time including a baron of beef weighing between 30 and 40 stone (560 lb) and a whole roasted buck. There were also twenty-one joints of roast beef, fifteen of pressed beef, seventeen galantines of veal, twenty-four game pies, fourteen large hams, twenty-eight tongues, fifteen turkeys, eight boars' heads, fifteen rounds of beef, ten legs and fourteen shoulders of mutton, seventy-two roast fowls, fifty-four pheasants, sixty-two partridges, twenty plum puddings and so on, making a total of 1,000 dishes, plus a 120 lb birthday cake.

One of the unique elements of extreme-aged cask ale is that it was a style that could not have developed in a commercial environment. Storing ale or beer on a large scale was developed by porter brewers in the mid-eighteenth century, and even the biggest casks at Belvoir Castle or Stowe House were dwarfed by the vast vats used by the London porter brewers, such as Barclay Perkins, where the largest stood 40 feet tall and measured 40 feet across at the widest part, giving a capacity of 3,300 barrels. But those vats were used to age maturing porter for only a year or two. Longer-aged ale was very occasionally found for sale: the *Times* in November 1859, for example, had an advertisement from a man in Clapham addressed to 'brewers and others' for 'about 65 barrels of three-year-old ale, perfectly sound and in brilliant condition. Has been moved three times in the past three months and each time has gone perfectly bright of its own according in a few days.' The price was only 23 shillings a barrel, however, less even than fresh table ale.

On the other hand, in February 1863 the *Bristol Mercury* carried an ad for 'a vat of 200 barrels of very superior old ale, vatted in 1857, to be sold at 48s per barrel, for cash.' Assuming this was brewed in October 1857 it was then five years and three months old. West Country drinkers were famous for their preference for old ale: a writer in the *Journal of the Society of Arts* in 1890 declared that, 'In the West of England and in Belgium this fashion of drinking old ale has not yet died out.' One of the few other commercial aged ales I have been able to find mention of, however, was from York, where, at a clearance sale at the Old Bird-In-Hand Hotel, Bootham, in October 1878, the departing landlord sold his complete brewing plant, horses, carriages, poultry, pigeons and 'One Puncheon of Fine 7 years' old STRONG ALE, in splendid condition' – a puncheon, in beer brewing, was a cask with a capacity of 72 gallons, equal to two barrels.

All of these, however, even the oldest commercial aged cask ales, were beardless youths compared to the ancient keeping ales made by the gentry and aristocracy in anticipation of their sons' coming-of-age celebrations. No commercial brewer could afford to keep an ale maturing for two decades. A nobleman such as the Duke of Portland, however, had the wealth to pay for the raw materials, the huge cellars in which to store a long-life ale undisturbed, the confidence to undertake a venture that would not pay off for more than two decades and a substantial brewing operation in existence, to supply his household staff and estate workers with what was still a necessity, daily beer and ale. Sometimes 100 people sat down to dine in the servants' hall at the duke's home, Welbeck Abbey, near Worksop, North Nottinghamshire, in the 1850s, and they were supplied with drink by a beer barrel on wheels that ran up and down the table. In 1879, servants at Trentham Hall, Staffordshire, home of the Dukes of Sutherland, were allowed four pints a day for men and two for women. That implies the Welbeck Abbey brewery, assuming the servants there received the same allowance, was producing perhaps seven barrels a week as a minimum. It would not be hard to switch that production for one week into making a super-strong ale for laying down, as happened at Welbeck in 1802, when the fourth Duke of Portland's second son, Lord George Bentinck, was born. One of many enormous casks in the Welbeck Abbey cellars was filled with ale, and Lord George's name and date of birth painted on it, ready for the contents to be given away to the duke's workers and tenants when Lord George came of age. (Though in this case, it appears, Lord George's ale was never given away, and remained in the cellars even after his death in 1848.)

There was, of course, a massive element of showing off involved in the production of such super-aged ales, and in the whole roast-ox, dinner-for-500 theatricals of an aristocratic coming of age, as well as a sense that this was part of the idea of noblesse oblige, the rich man in his castle's obligation to give the poor man at his gate a jolly good party occasionally. A coming-of-age celebration, complete with twenty-one-year-old ale, features in George Eliot's *Adam Bede*, written in 1859 but set in 1799. It is July, and everyone in the locality, farmers, farm workers and their families, have been invited to the celebrations for the twenty-first birthday of the 'young Squire', Captain Arthur Donnithorne, at Donnithorne Chase. The men are particularly keen. 'It is a time of leisure on the farm, that pause between hay and corn-harvest, and so the farmers and labourers in Hayslope and Broxton thought the captain did well to come of age just then, when they could give their undivided minds to the flavour of the great cask of ale which had been brewed the autumn after "the heir" was born, and was to be tapped on his twenty-first birthday.'

What was that flavour? The *Illustrated News* reported in February 1857 on 'Tapping the barrel of Lincoln Ale', which took place at the Duke of Newcastle's home, Cumber Park, not far from Welbeck Abbey, at the celebrations for the coming of age of his eldest son the Earl of Lincoln (celebrations delayed two years because of the Crimean War). The ale brewed when the earl was born had been 'placed in a butt and ceremoniously deposited in the cellars' at Clumber, then 'carefully attended to; and being now twenty-three years old, it resembles wine.' Extreme-aged ale was certainly very strong. In 1897, during a hearing by the Home Office committee on beer materials, the conversation turned to aged ales, and the committee chairman, Sidney Herbert, the Earl of Pembroke, who was then fifty-four, began reminiscing,

> Of course, as we are all aware, the old custom was to have so many casks of beer brewed when the eldest son was born and it was not opened till he came of age ... that beer was of a very intoxicating nature by the time it was used. Of course, it was made very strong: you can concentrate it ... I am not sure that the 21-years-old ale was a very wholesome drink when the twenty-one years was passed. It was extremely intoxicating.

The witness (Andrew Mansell, a farmer and barley-grower from Shifnall in Shropshire) added, 'But, of course, you would take it accordingly. You would drink such ale in champagne glasses; you would not drink it like beer.'

However, in 1880, William Gladstone, then serving as both Prime Minister and Chancellor of the Exchequer, had delivered the 'Free Mash Tun' budget, which removed all tax on malt, but brought in a tax on private brewers' output for the first time: if the house they lived in was worth more than £15 a year, they had to pay full duty on all the beer they brewed.

That meant great families like the Noels and the Wynns now had to pay tax up front if they wanted to lay down several hundred gallons of sledgehammer brew for the newborn heir's coming-of-age celebrations in a couple of decades' time. Not surprisingly, the practice of making extreme-aged ale seems to have gone into sharp decline (as did private brewing itself; by 1895 the number of licensed home brewers had fallen more than 80 per cent, from the 100,000 recorded in 1870 to just over 17,000).

Belvoir Castle is a good illustration of the decline and disappearance of extreme-aged cask ale. Under the castle were two ale cellars and the 'small beer cellar'. In the first half of the nineteenth century they were stuffed with casks; the smaller ale cellar, under the north terrace, held getting on for 6,000 gallons in a dozen or so vessels, each containing about 500 gallons. The larger cellar contained twenty-eight casks, the biggest of which, named after Robert de Todeni, the Norman knight who was made Lord of Belvoir after William the Conqueror's invasion in 1066, held 1,300 gallons – thirty-six barrels. Inside this cask, thirteen people were supposed to have dined. It bore a label, in the 1830s, with the date 16 May 1815, the day the then-Marquis of Granby, eldest son of the duke, was born and the cask filled. It was tapped on his coming of age in 1836, when his father, whose own massive celebrations had taken place in 1799, put on such an enormous party that 'not a labourer or wayfaring man within seven miles of the castle went to bed sober that night'. Even so, visitors to the castle were still being offered a wine-glass of the marquis' coming-of-age ale when they were shown around the cellars a year later, though the antiquarian Thomas Frognall Dibdin thought that 'the strength and the flavour of this barley broth were, to my palate, either decomposed or passed away.'

That Marquis of Granby (whose great-grandfather was the marquis who gave his name to so many pubs) became Duke of Rutland in 1857 and died unmarried in March 1888, to be succeeded as duke by his brother John. Just over a year later, in July 1889, the *Daily Telegraph* was reporting that the twenty-four-hogshead 'Robert de Todeni' and two other huge beer casks, with capacities of 13 hogsheads (702 gallons) and 8 hogsheads respectively, 'which have so long been the pride of the spacious cellar' at Belvoir Castle, had been 'removed from their traditional crypts', and 'at the present time poor "Robert de Todeni" is lying on its side near the stables of the Castle like a huge vessel stranded'.

The *Telegraph* wailed over the fact that

> the number of county families who continue to brew their own beer and to dispense it gratuitously to their tenants and farm-labourers is every year visibly diminishing. When so little is got out of the land as is the case nowadays, the landowner scarcely thinks it worthwhile to regale his poorer neighbours with eleemosynary [free] beer; and although in a few districts there might be some fine old English gentlemen who continue to follow the pleasant practice of tapping on the coming of age of the heir the hogshead of 'humming ale' which was brewed in the year when he was born, the custom has grown to one much more honoured in the breach than the observance.

There were still extreme-aged brews being tapped. In January 1885 the coming of age of the Honourable Gustavus Hamilton Russell, eldest son of Viscount Boyne of Brancepeth Castle in County Durham, was celebrated with an ox-roast and a dinner for 350 families. The contents of a 600-gallon cask of ale made in 1864, when young Gustavus was born, were distributed 'gratuitously to all comers' with the beef, while the band of the Northumberland Hussars played 'sweet music'. Charles Francis Kynaston Mainwaring of Oteley Park, Ellesmere, near Liverpool, welcoming some 1,500 to 2,000 locals to his twenty-first birthday celebrations in December 1892, invited them to taste his twenty-one-year-old ale (brewed 1871) before they dined, 'and many kind wishes for his future passed from mouth to mouth'.

Not everybody brewed their own. At the celebrations when Charles Grey, Viscount Howick, only son of Earl Grey, was twenty-one in December 1900, for the post-dinner toast to the Queen at Howick House in Northumberland 'there was provided Cambridge ale, brewed in the year 1874, and brought from College by Earl Grey when he completed his university career'. That would have been twenty-six-year-old ale from Trinity College, where Grey studied history and law; many colleges at Oxford and Cambridge also brewed their own ale and beer.

The First World War fifteen years later, and the massive rises in taxes on beer in Britain that conflict brought in, seems to have finally knocked on the head the extreme-aged 'young heir's twenty-first birthday' ale. The last two such brews I have been able to find records for were both made just before the war. Late in 1910 or early in 1911, a special ale was brewed at Wentworth Woodhouse, near Rotherham in Yorkshire, home of the Earl Fitzwilliam, for the birth of his eldest son, Peter Wentworth-Fitzwilliam, Viscount Milton. That ale was tapped at Lord Milton's twenty-first birthday celebrations on 31 December 1931, and drunk by guests who included more than 5,000 workmen, 'a large number of whom were coalminers employed by Lord Fitzwilliam'.

Less than four years after Lord Milton's birth, in May 1914, a son and heir was born to the Earl of Macclesfield. To mark the arrival of the new Viscount Parker, casks of strong ale were laid down in the cellars below the level of the moat at the family home, Shirburn Castle in Oxfordshire, to be drunk when he came of age. At the celebrations, on Monday 6 May 1935, tenants and employees of Lord Macclesfield from the villages of Shirburn and Stoke Talmage were entertained at supper. If – and presumably they did – they drank to Lord Parker's health in his twenty-one-year-old ale, I wonder how many were aware they were among the last enjoyers of a vanishing tradition.

10

The Tale of the Dimple Beer Mug

Loved and disliked in equal parts, and enjoying an unexpected renaissance in hipstery parts, despite being more than seventy years old, the dimpled beer mug is undoubtedly an icon of England.

It was invented in 1938 at the Ravenhead glassworks in St Helens, Lancashire, by an in-house designer whose name is now forgotten, and given the factory identity 'P404'. Although the dimple has its enemies, who dislike its weight and its thickness, it soon became extremely popular, and at a rough guess some 500 million have been manufactured since it was born.

The dimple had much competition; even in 1938, many pubs still served beer in the pottery mugs that George Orwell praised in his 'Moon Under Water' essay about his ideal pub, from the *Evening Standard* in 1946. Orwell declared that 'in my opinion beer tastes better out of china', but 'china mugs went out about 30 years ago [that is, during the First World War], because most people like their drink to be transparent'. However, two documentary films made just before Orwell's essay, *The Story of English Inns* from 1944 and *Down at the Local* from 1945, both show pint china mugs were still being used alongside glass ones, at least in country pubs. Orwell talked about the pottery beer mug as being strawberry-pink in colour, but they came in other shades (baby blue and a dark biscuit-beige, for example), all with white interiors and white handles, and also with transfer-print designs; however, the majority of pottery beer mugs appear, in fact, to have been of the kind known as mochaware, invented around the end of the eighteenth century, which have tree or fern-like patterns on the sides, made

Mr XXX, mascot of the Beer is Best campaign, leading his army of ten-sided beer mugs. (Picture courtesy of the British Beer and Pubs Association)

by a drop of acid dropped onto the glaze of the mug while it was still wet. Most mochaware pint beer mugs seem to have been blue, or beige and blue, with black-and-white bands. Many were made by T. G. Green of Church Gresley, South Derbyshire, while the plain coloured mugs were the speciality of Pountneys of Bristol. T. G. Green stopped producing mochaware at the outbreak of war in 1939, when it was apparently the last company still making mochaware beer mugs. It tried to revive the tradition in 1981, without success. The company closed in 2007.

Pewter mugs were pretty much obsolete by the middle of the twentieth century, though Orwell claimed that 'stout ... goes better in a pewter pot', and they were described as 'old-fashioned' even in 1900, when it was said to have been replaced by the glass mug, 'a thick, almost unbreakable article'. The problem, for publicans, was that their pewter pots kept being stolen, and they cost around ten times as much as china beer mugs. The better class of premises kept silver-plated pewter beer mugs and, to guard against theft, carved the name and address of the pub into the base. Glass was also cheaper – and, it was claimed, the working man at the end of the nineteenth century liked to have his mild beer served in a glass so that he could see it was bright, and not hazy or cloudy.

Fortunately for the beer-mug collector, after the Weights and Measures Act of 1878, drinking vessels used on licensed premises for draught beer or cider purporting to be a specific size – half-pint, pint or quart – had to bear an Official Stamp Number, either acid-etched or sand-blasted through a stencil. This system lasted, with tweaks, until 2007, and each district – county council, county borough and the like – had its own numbers, so that, for example, 19 was Derbyshire and 490 Bristol. They also carried the mark of the crown, and the initials of the reigning monarch of the time, something that had first been required by the Act 'for ascertaining the Measures for retailing Ale and Beer' that had become law under William III in 1700. (That Act covered vessels 'made of wood, earth, glass, horn, leather, pewter or of some other good and wholesome metal', suggesting the variety of drinking vessels you could expect in a Stuart inn or alehouse, and it also only mentions quarts and pints, suggesting the half-pint was illegal – or at least extremely rare.) It is thus often possible to tell roughly when an older beer mug was made, and roughly where, too. In 2007, when the CE, or 'Conformitée Européenne', mark replaced the old system (leading to the *Daily Mail* to declare, 'EU stealing the crown of the great British pint!'), it became easier to tell when a glass was made, but no simpler to find out where and by whom. Alongside the CE on the glass will be an 'M' and the last two digits of the year of manufacture, plus the identification number of the 'notified body' that verified that the container was an accurate measure. To indentify the notified body you have to go to the Nando website – nothing to do with peri-peri chicken, this stands for New Approach Notified and Designated Organisations.

Glasses specifically for drinking beer out of have been made in Britain since at least 1639, when a glasshouse (probably in Newcastle upon Tyne) owned by Sir Robert Mansell, who had acquired a monopoly on glass making, was selling beer glasses at a price half that of similar glasses imported from Venice. But such glasses were still expensive; in the 1660s, a glasshouse owned by the Duke of Buckingham in London was selling 'English Christall' beer glasses at 6d each, equivalent to more than £50 today. These were bowl-shaped glasses, with broad feet and heavy 'knops', the technical term for the ornamental knobs on the stem. Later, in the eighteenth century, beer and ale glasses became smaller and more delicate – at least in part because glass was taxed by weight from 1745 onwards – and were frequently decorated with fine engravings of hops, barley and so on. These engraved glasses held just 5 fl. oz (14cl) of strong beer or ale, or less. However, they were still restricted to the rich; when all the belongings of the late Earl of Grantham were auctioned off in February 1755, for example, among all the 'fine pictures, antique marble busts, large wardrobe of linnen, curious and magnificent collection of fine old Japan China, &c' for sale were fifty-three jelly glasses, eighteen water glasses, eighteen wine glasses and thirty beer glasses. Those beer glasses cost a hefty two to three shillings each, after tax. According to a letter in the *Pottery and Glass Trades Journal* in October 1879, because of the expense of glass, in the pub, inn or tavern, 'time was' that ale in a glass tumbler cost more than the same drink in a pewter mug: two pence per half pint, against one and a half pence.

It would take the invention of pressed glass, made by pressing semi-molten glass into an iron mould, before beer glasses could begin to come into the reach of the common drinker. Pressed glass was being made in Europe in the late eighteenth century, but the first patent for a commercial glass-pressing machine was granted in the United States in 1825 to John Palmer Bakewell, son of an English-born Pittsburgh glassmaker, Benjamin Bakewell. The first glass-pressing machine in Britain was installed at the Wordsley Flint Glass Works in Stourbridge in 1833, founded by Benjamin Richardson, whose firm became the first in the country to make mass-produced pressed-glass tumblers. Indeed, before pressed glass, tumblers – handle-less, footless glasses, tapering or straight-sided – and glass mugs with handles (called 'cans' by the glass makers), were difficult to produce. Moulded glass made their manufacture much easier.

However, in Britain glass remained relatively expensive until the abolition of the glass tax in 1845, which caused an 'immense' increase in the production of glass of all kinds. But even after that date, the evidence suggests that glass drinking vessels remained rare in pubs until the end of the Victorian period. While the catalogue of the Great Exhibition in Hyde Park in 1851 showed Thomas Webb of Platt's Glass Works, near Stourbridge, exhibiting 'ales' among his many types of glassware, from sugar bowls to vases, this appears to be the only specific mention of beer glasses among the more than thirty British glassware manufacturers there, and can be put alongside the porcelain porter mug exhibited by the Hanley pottery manufacturer Charles Meigh & Sons. There were more foreign exhibitors of beer glasses, from Prague and Prussia, than British. Three decades later, John Henry Henshall's painting *In the Pub* from 1882, otherwise known as *Behind the Bar* – a view of what is believed to be a pub in Old Street or Caledonian Road, London, from the staff side of the operation – appears to show only pewter pots on the shelves and in the sinks.

A decade later, however, there was suddenly a rush of evidence for the increasing popularity of beer in glass containers. In June 1894, the *Portsmouth Evening News* reported,

It has been noticed, says the Daily News, that the old-fashioned pewter pot has disappeared from public-houses and is replaced by beer glasses. In connection with the supply of these glasses – an enormous number of which is required –a serious complaint is heard from the glass trade in London. The stamping and verifying of the glasses costs a penny each – almost as much as the cost of production. Several County Councils in the north of England have been in the habit of allowing the makers to have the glasses stamped, under supervision of Council officials, on their own premises. This means a saving to the Councils, and they allow the manufacturers rebates of 30 or 40 per cent, which enables them to compete successfully with London makers. The fine machinery which the London County Council obtained to stamp the glasses is therefore now practically standing idle. A few months ago many thousands of glasses were being stamped every week, but now cheap stamped glasses are being imported from the north, the London glass trade is suffering in consequence and the Council is losing its fees. The Board of Trade has decided that it has no power to compel County Councils to stop the rebate system and do their own stamping.

The social researcher Charles Booth, in 1896, wrote in *Life and Labour of the People in London* that 'until comparatively recent years the publican's customers were very particular as to their ale being served in a "nice bright pewter pot" … the pot is, however, being now largely supplanted by the glass.' Two years later, in 1898, a witness to a parliamentary inquiry into the materials being used to brew beer talked about 'the alleged preference of the working man to have his beer in glasses' – which he denied, saying that it was the publicans leading the movement towards glass, because it was cheaper than pewter, and took up less space. All the same, the *Brewers' Journal* that year carried an article on brewing 'brilliant' beer, saying that there was a 'steadily increasing demand for light fresh beers … capable of withstanding the critical glass test', suggesting that the use of glass mugs and tumblers in pubs was indeed rising because of customer preference.

Although, under the 1872 Weights and Measures Act, all draught beer or cider sold in quantities of a half-pint or more had to be delivered to the customer in glasses bearing an official stamp, there was no such requirement governing the sale of quantities less than half a pint (10 fl. oz). Publicans asked for 'a half-pint' or 'a pint' or 'a quart' had to give their customer exactly that, in a stamped glass, but if asked for 'a glass' of beer, as long as it was less than half a pint, it could be any quantity. Most landlords, it would appear, kept a stock of unstamped 8 fl. oz beer glasses to supply those customers who asked for 'a glass' of ale or beer. The charge was a penny, but when David Lloyd George's budget of 1910 imposed big extra costs on brewers, pushing up the price of beer, a penny for 8 fl. oz was suddenly uneconomical. To keep the retail price of a 'glass of beer' at a penny, smaller glasses were needed. A 'pony', holding around a quarter of a pint, 5 fl. oz, was too small, so the publicans introduced a new beer glass holding four-thirteenths of a pint – 6.15 fl. oz – which was swiftly dubbed by customers the 'Lloyd George'. (The 'glass' of beer was finally outlawed by the Weights and Measures Act of 1963; since then, draught beer can only legally be sold in stamped glasses holding a third of a pint, half a pint or a pint – and, more recently, two thirds of a pint.)

Earlier Victorian beer glasses included rummers, or footed goblets, an attractive style that unfortunately died out. Glass beer mugs in late Victorian and Edwardian times seem to have been heavily ribbed, or cylindrical, while the tumblers were slightly slope-sided or conical. An advertisement for British-made beer tumblers from 1932 shows three different types: plain; with a rayed pattern on the bottom; and with internal ribs, in a style called 'Venetian'. By 1930 the Crystal Glass Company, a subsidiary of Bagley & Co. of Knottingley, West Yorkshire, was showing just one type of beer tumbler in its catalogue, the plain conical style, but three different types of glass beer mug: plain and cylindrical; with ribs or dentition around the base; and what was to become the first iconic beer glass, the ten-sided mug.

Who invented the ten-sided mug, where and exactly when – presumably in the 1920s – is not known. Jobling & Co. of Sunderland apparently also had ten-sided mugs in its catalogue, George Davidson of Gateshead may have made them and Ravenhead certainly did. But they soon became common; when the Brewers' Society began its 'Beer is Best' advertising campaign in 1933 to try to reverse falling beer sales, it swiftly started using the ten-sided mug in its advertising, with the campaign's mascot, 'Mr XXX', depicted as a cheery face inside a ten-sided pint glass with arms and legs. While most examples were made in standard clear glass, Bagley & Co. made some in yellow glass, and examples in amber glass are also known. Despite, as we shall see, being challenged and eventually being defeated by two rival designs of beer glass, the ten-sided mug was still being made by Ravenhead in St Helens as late as 1964, meaning it was in production for at least thirty-five years, and probably longer.

The first challenger to the ten-sided beer glass was the dimple mug. The design of the dimple, which seems particularly suited to reflecting and refracting the colour of amber beers, such as classic British ales, may have been inspired by the mugs with a flat hexagonal faceted exterior manufactured by Jobling & Co. in the 1920s and/or early 1930s. The dimple, despite being a Ravenhead design, was also picked up by other manufacturers, notably Dema of Chesterfield, in Derbyshire, which was Britain's largest domestic glassware manufacturer, though much less well-known to the public than Ravenhead. But it always had its enemies, and in 1990 it was the subject of a vicious attack by Design magazine.

What's short, fat, ugly and increasingly shunned by beer drinkers? The 'dimple' beer glass. You know the one; it's barrel-shaped with indentations, a handle and eco-unfriendly walls of thick glass. An early attempt at ergonomic design, the dimple is a miserable failure. No one's fingers actually seem to fit the depressions in the glass. The addition of a handle tacitly acknowledges this. Real ale and lager drinkers both dislike the dimple for the same reason; they don't think the glass shows off the drink to its best advantage. What they want is something taller, slimmer, and less weighty; a thin glass through which they can admire the colour and clarity of the beer. Bar staff aren't too keen on the dimple, either. It is heavy, awkward to store and does not stack and, because of its bulk and the projecting handle, difficult to wash, especially in the small sinks found in most bars.'

Over the next decade, the dimple mug did seem to be disappearing from pubs, as did the traditional question barstaff asked someone asking for a pint, 'Straight or handle?' When the only two makers of the dimple left in Britain, Ravenhead and Dema, went into receivership within months of each other in 2000 and 2001, the headlines insisted, 'Dimpled Pint Pots Doomed.' Fortunately for traditionalists, that hasn't happened, and in the past few years the dimple beer mug has actually become trendy in pubs and bars frequented by bearded hipsters. Even the 'straight or handle?' question has returned, at least in some bars. Today, however, your dimpled pint glass is most likely to have been made in China, by someone like the Zibo Hondao Trading Co. Ltd of Shandong, Bengbu Longyu Glass Products of neighbouring Anhui or the Shanghai Jingsheng Glass Co. Ltd, minimum order 100,000 glasses, cost FOB as low as 20p a glass, depending on order size.

The third 'Great British beer glass' – though personally it's one I hate as much as others dislike the dimple – was invented by a largely unsung giant of twentieth-century British design: Alexander Hardie Williamson. You may never have heard of him, but it is very likely you have drunk out of one or more of the glasses he designed on thousands of occasions. Hardie Williamson, who was born in 1907, had designed for Bagley & Co. in the 1930s, began designing glassware for United Glass, parent company of Ravenhead in 1944, and within a few years produced a host of simple design classics that are, in many cases, still with us today: the champagne saucer, picked up and personalised by Showerings as the Babycham glass, first made in 1948; the Paris wine goblet, designed in 1952; the 'Waterloo' half-pint goblet, as seen in Newcastle Brown Ale ads; the 'New Worthington' stemmed goblet, the Harp lager tankard and more. But his most widely produced design, still to be found in pubs almost everywhere, was the iconic Nonik tumbler, a slightly conical beaker with a bulge around an inch below the rim, first made by Ravenhead in 1948 and given the product number P708. The bulge near the top was intended to keep the rims from being chipped or nicked by rubbing or banging together in the glass washer or on the shelf – hence the name, from 'No Nick' – and had the added advantage that the bulge made it easier for the drinker to hold on to their pints when the glass was slippery than with straight-sided tumblers. Unfortunately, it's irredeemably ugly, with what *Design* magazine called its 'unsightly bulge'.

That has not, however, prevented it from becoming probably Britain's most ubiquitous glass. Like the dimple, the Nonik was quickly copied by other manufacturers: Dema had the style in its catalogue by 1952, under the slightly altered name 'Nonic'. Given that the glasses were produced for pubs during the last four years of the reign of George VI, there must, somewhere, be examples of Nonik/Nonic glasses stamped 'GR', though their thinness was always going to make them rarer survivors than the heavier, thicker dimples and ten-sided mugs, despite their being produced in enormous quantities. It has been estimated that 60 million beer glasses are supplied to British pubs, clubs and other drinking establishments every year (which implies that every establishment is breaking two to three a day). Let us take a very broad-brush guess and say that over the years a quarter of all beer glasses used in British pubs have been either dimples or Noniks/Nonics, with the rest tulips, straight-sided beakers, other types of tankards and so on. That would mean more than a billion individual Noniks and dimples have clattered over British bartops since the 1940s – and both look like it will be a long time before they are pensioned off.

11

The Dove, Hammersmith – a Tiny Mystery

The Dove in Upper Mall, Hammersmith, is one of London's favourite riverside pubs, famous for good beer, for a fine view of the annual Oxford versus Cambridge Boat Race and for what is supposed to be the tiniest public bar in Britain, at just 4 feet 2 inches wide and 7 feet 10 inches long. This is the story of that tiny bar, a tale of deceit and mystery.

The pub's popularity means a raft of mentions in guidebooks, with most of the 'facts' printed about it being demonstrably wrong. At least two guides to riverside pubs claim Charles II and his mistress Nell Gwyn used to visit the Dove, which would have been difficult without a time machine, as it wasn't built until around sixty years or more after Charles II died. Another popular national guide says the pub was 'licensed in 1740 as the Dove's [*sic*] coffee house' (it wasn't), and James 'Thompson' (*sic* – it was Thomson) composed 'Rule Britannia' in an upstairs room (he didn't – in fact he didn't 'compose' it at all. Thomas Arne composed the tune and Thomson wrote the words, most probably at his home in Kew).

How the Dove came to have such a tiny bar was explained by George Izzard, the pub's landlord from 1931 to 1965. He wrote one of the best 'landlord's memoirs', *One for the Road*, and he made the Dove a magnet for celebrities from Ernest Hemingway to Alec Guinness (who drank Guinness) to Dylan Thomas (whose usual order was mild-and-bitter, according to Izzard).

Until the time of his predecessors at the pub, Alfred and Elizabeth Mayes, the Dove – then called the Doves – was a one-bar beerhouse, licensed to sell beer only, not wine and spirits,

The Dove, Hammersmith (then still the Doves), when the landlord was Samuel Richardson Gamble – the name on the (birdless) signboard – sometime between 1874 and January 1881, the month the licence was handed over to Henry Thomas Saunders. The window to what became the smallest public bar in Britain is on the right of the door. (Author's collection)

Izzard wrote in *One for the Road*. The Mayeses, who came to the Dove in 1911, wanted to apply to the licensing magistrates to turn it into a fully licensed pub and sell the more profitable whisky, gin and rum alongside the four-ale. But the law said a pub could only have a full licence if it had two bars.

Putting a second bar in meant structural alterations, and structural alterations to a pub also required the permission of the licensing magistrates. However, it could be dangerous to ask the licensing bench for leave to make structural alterations: they might demand, as the price of permission, that a landlord make even more costly upgrades, such as new toilets. Even worse, in the early decades of the twentieth century, licensing benches were proactively closing pubs and beerhouses deemed 'surplus'. If the Mayeses drew attention to the Dove, the magistrates might come along and decide this little out-of-the-way beerhouse near the Stamford Brook creek needed shutting, not improving.

What to do? The Mayeses, Izzard wrote, decided on a cunning plan. Next door to the pub was a boatyard run by Mrs Mayes' brothers, the Coles. They would ask the Coles to build a prefabricated saloon bar in their boatyard, sneak the parts into the Dove late one evening and erect it when no one was about: '... the bar had only to be screwed down and the whole operation could be carried through in complete silence. The Cole brothers did their stuff. The new bar was built, spirited into the front door and screwed into place without anyone a penny the wiser.'

The following Brewster Sessions (the annual meeting of the licensing magistrates), Mr Mayes, landlord of the now two-bar Doves, applied for and was granted his spirits licence without the slightest difficulty, Izzard wrote. The tiny new compartment to the right of the Dove's front door stayed as a designated saloon bar, where beer cost a penny a pint more, until Izzard decided he would make much more money turning the main bar into the saloon, and changing the far smaller space, just 33 square feet, into the public bar, which is how it remains today.

It's a terrific story, and there is only one problem with it. The Dove never was a beerhouse, it has always had a full licence, and there was no need for the Mayeses to have a second bar built. It is true that the Licensing Consolidation Act of 1910 stated that a pub had to have two separate public rooms to be able to sell spirits. But the Act also said that this rule did not apply for any premises that had had an on-licence from before 1872. The Dove's history as licensed premises went back much further than that – indeed, it predated the Beerhouse Act of 1830, which brought in beer-only licences and saw tens of thousands of new drinking outlets open across the country.

The London County Council Survey of London of 1915

described the Dove, and its adjoining neighbour at 17 Upper Mall, a private house called The Seasons, as dating architecturally from 'the middle or early part of the eighteenth century' and being probably one building originally, or two cottages under one roof. The Survey suggests, though with no evidence at all, that there may be a link between the Dove and two cottages 'and a grass orchard' by the riverside listed in the local manor records between 1678 and 1718, but even if they were on the same site the Dove, architecturally, must be a rebuilding.

Thomas Faulkner's *Historical and Topographical Account of Fulham; Including the Hamlet of Hammersmith* from 1813 says the Scottish poet James Thomson wrote part of 'Winter', the last section in his poetic cycle *The Seasons*, 'in the Dove coffee-house', adding that 'he was in the habit of frequenting the room when the Thames was frozen and the surrounding country was covered in snow. This fact is well authenticated and many people visit the house to this present day.' It is on this claim that 17 Upper Mall is called The Seasons: the 1915 Survey of London says that 'it has been suggested that the room occasionally occupied by Thomson may have been the upper room of number 17 before it was divided from the inn.'

Thomson, whom the Dictionary of National Biography calls 'a keen and practised drinker' (you go, Jimbo), wrote *The Seasons* between 1725 and 1730. It was not until 1736 that he was living in the area, in a cottage in Kew Foot Lane, Richmond, from where he would walk the 9 or 10 miles into London, with 'the Doves inn at Hammersmith as his customary watering hole', the DNB says. This is at least in part anachronistic; the premises were still called 'the Dove coffee house' at the end of the eighteenth century, and the Dove never properly turned into the Doves until around the middle of the nineteenth century.

Thomson wrote the patriotic *Alfred: A Masque*, which features 'Rule Britannia', in 1740, though there is no evidence he wrote the song at the Dove. He heavily revised *The Seasons* in 1743, and might have done this while at the Dove on his way to or from London, but again, there is no evidence. What is known is that, after walking one hot summer evening in August 1748

from central London as far as Hammersmith, Thomson took
a boat for the remainder of his journey home to Kew, caught
a chill, which turned into a fever, and died a few days after,
aged forty-eight. His wake, the DNB says, was 'as drunken as
Thomson could have wished'.

If Faulkner and the DNB are right, then the Dove may have
been around, and serving customers, as early as the 1730s, at
least; I don't know what their sources are, however. The first
documented evidence for the Dove's existence does not come
until November 1790, when the local manorial court rolls
record that Julian Bere, spinster, died 'seized of the Doves [*sic*]
coffee house then in the occupation of James Cade'. Two years
later, Montague Beer, evidently a relative of Julian, was shown
in the manorial records as taking up the ownership of 'a coffee
house called the Dove, near Chiswick'.

The Dove was then occupied by 'James Thompson or his
undertenant'. 'James' Thompson was possibly a mistake for
John Thompson, then owner of the brewery down the road in
Chiswick that later became Fuller, Smith & Turner, because in
November 1796 the manorial records say Beer surrendered 'the
Dove coffee house by the creek' to the use of John Thompson
of Chiswick, and 1796 is when Fuller's records say the brewery
acquired the Dove.

The fact that the Dove was called a coffee house, even though
the involvement of Thompson shows it was selling beer as well,
suggests a rather more upmarket or exclusive establishment than
a simple riverside alehouse. Coffee houses, in London at least,
in the eighteenth century, were places where the middle classes
met, where (expensive, highly taxed) newspapers were made
available, where wits tried to outdo each other in cleverness,
where politicians plotted and where businessmen transacted
their affairs.

Hammersmith at this time was still fairly rural: there were
fields and orchards on almost every side. However, the district
did attract upper-class visitors. In a later book Thomas Faulkner
said the Seasons, next door to the Dove, was used by Augustus
Frederick, Duke of Sussex (1773–1843), sixth son of George

III and Queen Victoria's favourite uncle, as a 'smoking box', where he would 'smoke the social tube' in the garden next door to the river. He was not the first royal to visit Upper Mall: Queen Catherine, the widow of Charles II, spent her summers in a house further along from where the Dove now is between 1686 and 1694 (which may be where the canard that Charles II himself visited the area comes from), and her brother-in-law James II would regularly call on her.

According to the 1965 *A History of Hammersmith*, the Dove was still called the Dove Coffee House in 1820, when it was one of the places where a petition in support of Queen Caroline, the estranged wife of the newly crowned George IV, could be signed: Caroline was living in Hammersmith, and being visited by Whig politicians who were supporting her as a way of embarrassing the Tory government. By the time of Pigot's trade directory of 1826/7, where it is listed under 'Taverns and Public Houses', the place is simply called the Dove – no mention of coffee.

At least one source claims the change of name to the Doves happened in 1860 after 'the artist repainting the sign was overcome with enthusiasm and put in two birds instead of one'. In a directory of 1845, however, and again in the 1851 census, it is called the Doves, plural, while in Simpson's directory of 1863 it is called the Dove, singular, again. A watercolour painting by J. T. Wilson from 1867, however, shows the riverside signboard calling the pub the Doves. (It also shows an advertising board for 'neat wines', confirming, if it were needed, that the Dove/Doves had a full licence even then).

Although the pub continued to be called the Doves on its signs, the licensing records for Hammersmith and Fulham, which begin in 1873, show the pub, with its full licence, was always listed as the Dove, singular. When, in 1948, George Izzard discovered what the name had been originally, he decided to revert to the old style, and the pub has been the Dove ever since. (Ironically, the dustjacket of Izzard's autobiography, published in 1959, shows a photograph of the pub from the river with the name in huge letters on the signboard as 'THE DOVES'.)

But if the Dove/Doves already had a full licence, why did the

Mayeses feel they had to have a second bar? Alfred Mayes died in 1921, and his widow Elizabeth carried on at the pub until her death in 1930. George Izzard must have heard the 'wanted to upgrade the licence' story from one of the locals who knew the secret of how the new saloon bar had been installed, perhaps second-hand, and who did not know the pub could sell wines and spirits even before the new bar was snuck in one night.

My guess is that the Mayeses had been told that the 1910 Licensing Consolidation Act said only two-bar pubs could have full licences, and, not realising they were safe from this rule because of the Dove's age, had panicked, thinking they might have their full licence taken away, and decided to secretly upgrade the pub so that it complied with the law. Alfred Mayes already had a mark on his record; in 1916 he had been convicted for serving alcohol after hours. Perhaps he felt, because of this, under a particular obligation to be seen to obey the regulations.

Whatever, the tiny but 'delightful' bar (to quote Camra's guide to London pubs of special interest), albeit a twentieth-century addition, only increases the attraction of this eighteenth-century riverside pub. It deserves all its places in the guidebooks, with its black oak settles, stone floors and Thames-side terrace (indeed, in the days of named London telephone exchanges, the pub's telephone number was actually RIVerside 5405, and riverside is what it still is, with the first part of the current number, 8748, being 8RIV).

It's only a pity the guidebooks can't get their facts right, but each author seems to copy and paste the errors of the previous writer, and introduce an error of their own at the same time. You can trace the development of the Charles and Nell myth, for example, from a pamphlet about the pub written in the 1950s saying the pair 'stayed in the district', through to the current nonsense that the Merry Monarch and the orange-seller actually drank at the yet-to-be-built pub.

12

The Most Notorious Brewer in History

In the autumn of 1775, Henry Thrale, owner of one of the biggest porter breweries in London, took his family on a trip across the English Channel to Paris. With them went Dr Samuel Johnson, the dictionary-writer and author, one of the great literary figures of eighteenth-century England, who had been good friends with Thrale and his wife Hester for ten years. In Paris the Thrales and Johnson toured the sights, visited palaces, churches and gardens, and educated themselves with a trip to a manufacturer of mirrors. Henry Thrale also called in on Paris's biggest brewer, a man called Antoine-Joseph Santerre, taking Johnson with him.

Johnson's notes of the visit say that although Santerre's Hortensia brewery, in the Rue de Reuilly, part of the Faubourg St Antoine, was the largest of seventeen brewing establishments in the city, it brewed just 4,000 barrels a year. This was barely a twentieth of the annual output at the time of Thrale's own Anchor brewery in Southwark. Johnson also recorded that Santerre made his own malt, and used about as much malt per barrel as Thrale did; yet he sold his beer for the same price as Thrale, though he paid no malt tax, and only half as much beer tax.

Johnson – an oak-hard Tory, who had recently produced a pamphlet attacking the American colonists for their rebelliousness against the British crown – would have been horrified to learn that he was shaking hands with a man who, fourteen years later, would aid the mobs of the Faubourg St Antoine in their successful assault of 14 July on the Bastille, and who, four and

Antoine Santerre fleeing from the Vendeans in 1793, by Jean-Baptiste LeSueur. (Musée Carnavalet, Paris)

a half years after that, would escort Louis XVI from his prison to the guillotine.

Johnson was five years dead when the French Revolution broke out, but Hester Thrale remembered Santerre and suggested after the Parisian brewer became notorious that he had become a revolutionary because of an incident that happened around the time the Thrales were in Paris. A fine horse belonging to Santerre got in the way of a royal procession and an officer in the army drew out his pistol and shot the animal dead, an act that, according to Hester, filled Santerre with anger.

Antoine-Joseph was the third of six children born to Augustin Santerre, a brewer from the small town of Saint Michel in Thiérache, just 7 miles from the modern Belgian border in Northern France. He had moved to Paris in 1747, buying in December that year the Magdeleine brewery in the Rue d'Orléans, in the Faubourg Saint-Marcel, from a widow called Marguerite Poussy. Four months later he married his cousin Marie-Marguerite, whose family were also brewers from Cambrai, another town in north-east France. Augustin's business later moved to Rue Censier, on the Left Bank, where Antoine was born in 1752 and where he served his apprenticeship as a brewer. Antoine's parents both died in 1770, but in 1772, aged only twenty, he was able to buy the Hortensia brewery in the Faubourg St Antoine from a Monsieur Acloque for 65,000 francs.

Santerre was fascinated by *la bière Anglais*; his brother François, who also ran breweries in and around Paris, visited London and studied brewing techniques there, bringing some back to France, where Antoine adopted them. According to his biographer, Antoine Carro, writing in 1847, Antoine Santerre was the first brewer in France to use a thermometer to measure accurately the temperature of his mashtun, rather than the 'uncertain gropings' of before, when brewers would judge the temperature by how long they could hold their hand in the water. He was the first to dry his malt English-style, with coke rather than wood, coke being so little known in France, Carro said, that it did not even have a name in French; Santerre called it *'l'escarbille'*, 'cinders', the name under which coke was apparently 'long known' subsequently by French brewers. Santerre was also the first French brewer to install a steam engine in his brewery, which replaced four horses, Carro said. In addition he and his brother analysed English ale and porter so successfully that they were able to 'perfectly imitate them'; they became, for a long time, the only brewers in France to make the two English styles, in a brewery run by François in Sevres, some 6 miles from the heart of Paris.

Santerre, 5 feet 4 inches tall, with brown eyes – 'the left significantly smaller than the right', according to Carro – and chestnut hair, 'always well powdered and arranged with care', was hugely popular with the poor people of the Faubourg St

Antoine, one of Paris's more industrialised districts. In part, it was said, this was because of his bluff personality and what was described as 'a sonorous, easy eloquence', and in part because he gave out large sums of money in the district, as well as handing out provisions; during one famine he distributed bread to the poor worth 300,000 francs, and in the winter of 1792 it was said that he bought up all the rice he could find and 'flocks of sheep' and turned the brewery coppers into stewpots, with his workmen preparing enormous stews for the poor. He was famous as a horseman, and was reckoned, according to later accounts, to be the second-best rider in the kingdom after Louis-Philippe, Duc d'Orleans. All the horses in the brewery stables were *'magnifique'*, according to Carro, including one giant called 'Sans pareil', and Santerre had a reputation for being able to take animals rejected elsewhere for being too rebellious and taming them for work between the shafts.

In May 1789, as Louis XVI struggled to control a financial crisis caused by the costs of supporting the American Revolution and the failure to properly tax the French nobility, the king had convened a meeting of France's ancient parliament, the Estates-general. It quickly became clear that the 'Third Estate', the representatives of the people, wanted a great deal of power to be surrendered by the king before they would agree to any solution to the problem of funding the state. In the middle of July the tensions between the king, completely unwilling to see his privileges and power eroded, and the Third Estate, who had formed themselves into a National Assembly, exploded into violence. The Parisian mob, fearful that troops would be used against the National Assembly, stormed the royal fortress of the Bastille, on the edge of the Faubourg St Antoine, to get hold of the gunpowder that was stored there. Santerre led the attackers (although his later detractors disputed this), was supposedly wounded in the assault, and cemented himself in the hearts of the local people as a hero of the revolution. When, very soon after, an armed people's militia was formed, the National Guard, Santerre was given command of the Faubourg St Antoine battalion.

Over the next three years Santerre's brewery became a meeting place for the most revolutionary group in French politics, the Jacobins, who were led by men such as Robespierre and Danton. As France struggled to turn itself from absolutism into something closer to a constitutional monarchy, Santerre was involved in a couple of unsuccessful insurrections evidently bent on eliminating royal power completely. Then, on 10 August 1792, he led an armed mob many thousands strong from the Faubourg St Antoine into the Tuileries, the royal palace. (Strangely, one of Louis' staunchest defenders on the day of the Tuileries invasion was another brewer, a National Guard commander called Acloque – the son of the man from whom Santerre bought the Hortensia brewery, whose own brewhouse was in the Faubourg St Marceau.) The invasion of the Tuileries culminated in the flight of Louis XVI into the arms of the National Assembly; the massacre of the Swiss Guards; Santerre's elevation to commander-in-chief of the whole of the Paris National Guard with the rank of general; and, six weeks later, Louis XVI's overthrow and arrest.

As commander of the National Guard, Santerre was in charge of the ex-king during his imprisonment and trial, and it was Santerre who came to take Louis to the guillotine on 21 January 1793, allegedly telling him, 'Monsieur, it's time to go.' What happened when the ex-king mounted the steps to the guillotine in the Place de la Revolution has been argued over for two centuries. Louis turned to the huge crowd, declared his innocence and forgave his enemies. Before he could say any more, the military drummers around the scaffold started up, drowning out any further words, and Louis was forced to lay his head upon the block, the blade of the guillotine descending upon his neck. Most records say it was Santerre the brewer who ordered the drummers to begin playing, with at least one account claiming that Santerre had shouted out as the king tried to speak that he had not brought Louis 'there to declaim, but to die.' For that he was declared by the English politician Edmund Burke to be a 'nefarious villain', while others called him 'inhuman', 'a monster of cruelty', 'infamous' and 'execrable'.

There are at least three other candidates for the man who told the drummers to start up and block the sound of Louis' last speech, however. Santerre's family later claimed that the brewer actually silenced the drums, to enable Louis to speak to the people, and that General Jean Francois Berruyer, the army commander in Paris, who was in sole command at the execution, ordered the drums to begin beating again. Berruyer allegedly said later that as Louis began speaking, 'Santerre did not interfere, and if I had not ordered an immediate drum roll to smother the voice of the tyrant, I do not know what would have happened!' Some have claimed it was Santerre's aide-de-camp, a comic actor called Dugazon, who gave the order. Another tradition says that the man who exclaimed, 'Strike the drums!' was Berruyer's chief of staff, Louis Charles Antoine de Beaufranchet, Comte d'Oyat – whose mother was Marie-Louise O'Murphy, the former fifteen-year-old mistress to Louis XV, and whose father, it was alleged, was Louis XV himself, which would mean the Comte was Louis XVI's illegitimate great-uncle.

All the same, years later, in 1802, Santerre told an English visitor to Paris called (somewhat ironically) Mr King, who had arranged an interview ostensibly to see a 'brewing machine' the Frenchman had invented, that he had indeed ordered the drums to roll.

He said it was expected there would be a cry of mercy, and he had received peremptory orders to fire on those who called for mercy; he saw several well-known aristocrats surrounding the scaffold and preparing to cry out; an immense body of Marseillois watched them, and meant to answer it with a contrary exclamation. If this contest had ensued, thousands would have perished in it; he perceived what was passing and, from the most humane motives, and not to drown the King's voice and distress him in his last few moments, he ordered the drums to beat; and, though the duty of seeing the King's sentence executed devolved on him, it was impossible he could rejoice at an event that, however necessary, was distressing and lamentable; he deplored it as much as any man in France.

All the while Santerre was in charge of the National Guard in Paris, his brewery business was still running; in April 1793 he obtained a tax rebate of 40,603 francs in beer duty on the grounds that the beer made by his brewery in the years 1789 to 1791 had been supplied free to National Guards and the 'patriotic populace'. Shortly before, Santerre had brought ridicule upon himself by having placards put up around Paris urging people to get rid of their pets, saying that the city's cats and dogs ate enough food to feed 1,500 men. One joker urged him to get rid of all the sparrows from Paris as well.

Meanwhile the Vendée, in the far west of France, had exploded into revolt, and Santerre was appointed a brigadier-general and placed in charge of an army of 14,000 men sent from Paris to put the counter-revolutionaries down. Unfortunately, he was a terrible general: he was beaten in battle at Saumur on 9 June 1793 and Coron on 18 September 1793 (his enemies claimed Santerre ran away the first time the Vendeans opened fire on the Parisian guards), and two-thirds of the revolutionary troops were killed. Santerre was recalled to Paris in disgrace, faced with accusations from his cavalry commander, Joachim Murat (later one of Napoleon's most loyal supporters, who became Napoleon's brother-in-law and, from 1808 to 1815, King of Naples), of drunkenness, ignorance and cowardice; there were also claims that he was a secret Orleanist, supporter of the Duc d'Orleans, cousin of Louis XVI, now calling himself Phillipe Egalité but who was suspected of wanting the throne of France for himself. Santerre was sent to prison, where he remained until the fall of Robespierre in July 1794.

His enemies had joked at the time of his military failures that the brewer-general had '*n'eut de Mars que la bière*', a pun on '*bière de Mars*', French for 'March beer'. No longer a general, Santerre tried to return to brewing. His wife, however, had fled Paris, leaving the brewery shuttered up, and the business never recovered. In January 1796 it was sold to a Monsieur Cousin. Santerre managed to obtain a post buying horses abroad for the Directory, the post-Terror government of France, and went into property speculation, at first successfully. His influence with the

people was still great enough that when Napoleon Bonaparte
enacted his coup of 18 Brumaire in 1797, which put Bonaparte
over France as 'First Consul', he sent a message to Santerre
saying that if the Fauberg St Antoine was not kept quiet, 'I will
have him shot before another hour passes over his head'.

All the same, in 1800 Napoleon restored Santerre's rank
of Brigadier-General to him, albeit only on half-pay pension.
Santerre carried on buying and selling property. However, in
1805 he made a stretch too far, buying a chateau in western
Normandy for 1.8 million francs. The expenses of the purchase
bankrupted him. He was forced to live with his eldest son in an
apartment in Paris, hiding from his creditors.

By 1807 Santerre was losing his grip: he was convinced the
people of the Vendée were after him with an iron cage in which
they wished to roast him alive. Yet he was still able to write a
book, *L'Art du Brasseur* ('The Art of Brewing), dedicated to
his sons, Augustin, Alexandre and Théodore; it covered every
aspect of the brewing process, from malting onwards, including
the vital role of supervision of the workforce. 'You have to be
the inspector of everyone, and without pause, if you want to
succeed completely,' Santerre told his sons. The following year
he suffered a stroke, and he died in February 1809, aged fifty-
five. Not one friend came to his funeral.

After his death, and particularly after the fall of Napoleon and
the restoration of the Bourbons to the throne of France, Santerre
continued to be regarded as the most villainous brewer that ever
lived for his alleged actions at the execution of Louis XVI. He
is also the real-life brewer that appears in the most works of
fiction: Victor Hugo, Antony Trollope, Baroness Orczy (creator
of the Scarlet Pimpernel), Alexander Dumas and ten or a dozen
more authors have included Santerre as a character in novels set
at the time of the French Revolution.

13

The Origins of Binge Drinking

To binge, the *Oxford English Dictionary* reveals, was originally a Lincolnshire (and, it implies, East Midlands generally) dialect word meaning 'to soak (a wooden vessel)'.

The metaphorical extension of meaning from soaking wood to soaking yourself was an easy journey, and by 1854 a book called *A Glossary of Northamptonshire Words* had recorded this figurative use for the word, 'A man goes to the alehouse to get a good binge, or to binge himself.'

A dictionary of slang published in 1889 said of 'binge' that it was used at Oxford to mean 'a big drinking bout'. By the early twentieth century the word was being used for parties at which large amounts of drink were consumed, with no particular sense that there was anything to criticise; the *OED* has a quote from 1922, 'This is only a binge ... just a jolly old bachelor-party.'

The word also took on secondary meanings, 'to encourage', and 'to liven up', as in a quote from the children's novel *National Velvet*, published in 1935. 'The information having been looked over and binged up here and toned down there ... Reuter sent round the world the following message ...'

It was probably from this sense of 'livened up' that General (later Field Marshal Lord) Montgomery used to ask his officers in the Second World War, 'Are you 100 per cent full of binge?', according to *The Times* in 1942. Monty meant, apparently, to ask if they were full of spirit in the metaphorical sense – zing – and confidence in their own ability and fitness, rather than whisky-ed up to the hairline. It was not a use that caught on.

'Binge drinking' and 'binge drinker' as phrases are comparatively modern, and come a while after the invention of the concept of 'binge eating' by psychiatrists to describe problems such as bulimia. 'Eating binge' occurs in the 1930s; the *OED* first finds 'binge eating' used in the *Psychiatric Quarterly* in 1959.

The *Times* first printed the expression 'binge drinker' in 1969, in an article about alcoholics headlined 'Call to help men who drink 30 pints a day'. The piece contrasts steady 'heavy' drinkers, who 'might not recognise themselves as alcoholics' when they heard the 'dramatic stories of the "binge drinkers"'. A 'binge drinker' as used by psychiatrists was someone who 'goes off periodically and gets himself very drunk, perhaps for days on end, but between bouts he may drink little or nothing, and so can argue that he is not addicted.'

The idea of 'binge drinking' as episodic heavy drinking continued through into the 1980s and the early 1990s. In 1988, for example, Douglas Hurd, then Home Secretary, 'called for action against crime by "binge drinkers, drunken drivers and people who down 12 pints and get into fights"'. Presumably the writer did not mean the binge drinkers should be taking the action against crime ... Anyway, the same year, Jancis Robinson, in her book *On the Demon Drink*, sub-titled *For the First Time Objective Assessment of Alcohol from Someone Who Loves It*, was able to say, 'Because much less guilt attaches to social drinking in this country than in, say, Sweden, binge drinking is far less common (although it is notable that the more Nordic the area in Britain, the more prevalent it is).'

Even in 1992 a report in the *Times* could write, 'Four out of ten 18-to-24 year-olds drink more than the "safe" limits (21 units a week for men and 14 units for women), a higher proportion than any other age group. *This is mostly social rather than binge drinking* [my emphasis]. Young people are the most socially active segment of the community and much social life, especially in colleges and universities, revolves around pubs, clubs and bars.'

By the early 1990s, however, when the idea of recommended weekly limits on alcohol drinking was gaining wider use, 'binge drinking' began to be specifically defined by alcohol researchers as 'drinking over half the recommended units for one week in a single session' – a definition, of course, with no known rationale or evidence to back it up.

Then in 1995 the government report *Sensible Drinking* pushed successfully for moving away from recommended weekly limits to recommended daily limits, and 'binge drinking' was redefined again as drinking twice the recommended daily limit in a single session; again, there was little real rationale for this change in definition that cut the amount of alcohol in a 'binge' by almost a quarter.

Since 'twice the recommended daily limit' could be as low as three or three and a half pints of beer for men and two and a half medium-sized glasses of wine for women, this suddenly put an awful lot of ordinary people's ordinary nights out into the 'binge' category.

Our nannying government likes to run advertising campaigns meant to make us fearful of just how many 'units' are in every glass we drink. But what you won't hear from the government is that between 2004 and 2013 there was an 18.9 per cent fall in alcohol consumption per head and consumption in 2013 was at its lowest level this century. Violent crime linked to alcohol had fallen by 32 per cent since 2004 and by 47 per cent since 1995. Since 2005, the number of men officially 'binge drinking' (a concept, as we have seen, based on dubious methodology and out-of-thin-air figures) has fallen by 17 per cent; the number of women binge drinking has fallen by 23 per cent; and binge drinking among sixteen- to twenty-four-year-olds had fallen by 31 per cent among men and by 34 per cent among women. Looks like the old-fashioned Lincolnshire soak is less and less popular.

Havisham's Kentish Ales – Beer in Literature

The benefits of a Liberal Arts education are many – and one is that by studying great literature, you can uncover a surprising amount of information about beer and brewing.

Take James Joyce's *Ulysses*, for example, undoubtedly one of the greatest books of the twentieth century. Here we find a name check to Lord Ardilaun and Lord Iveagh, great-great-grandsons of the first Arthur Guinness, founder of the eponymous brewing concern at St James's Gate in Dublin, and learn how Guinness is made. At one point Joyce has a character bring

> a crystal cup full of the foaming ebon ale which the noble twin brothers Bungiveagh and Bungardilaun brew ever in their divine alevats, cunning as the sons of deathless Leda. For they garner the succulent berries of the hop and mass and sift and bruise and brew them and they mix therewith sour juices and bring the must to the sacred fire and cease not night or day from their toil, those cunning brothers, lords of the vat.

Well, perhaps that's not really how it's done. But beer, brewing, breweries and brewers do pop up surprisingly often in the very best novels. You will discover in one of the great books of the nineteenth century, Thomas Hardy's *The Mayor of Casterbridge*, an excellent recipe for home-brewed ale of the sort made in country pubs in the West Country of England early in the nineteenth century.

Mr Bung the brewer and his son Master Bung, drawn by John Tenniel (1820–1914) in 1851 for the original Victorian Happy Families game. (Author's collection)

The Three Mariners was far from spacious, despite the fair area of ground it covered ... this being at a time before home-brewing was abandoned by the smaller victuallers, and a house in which the twelve-bushel strength was still religiously adhered to by the landlord in his ale, the quality of the liquor was the chief attraction of the premises, so that everything had to make way for utensils and operations in connection therewith.

'The twelve-bushel strength' meant 12 bushels of malt – one and a half quarters by volume, about 500 lb in weight – per imperial barrel, 36 gallons, of ale. This would give a heady brew indeed, north of 10 or 11 per cent alcohol even at the reduced efficiencies a small pub brewer in the time of the Kings George would be capable of. We know what the 'strong-beer' of Casterbridge (the name Hardy gave to Dorchester, county town of Dorset) was like, because he describes it in another novel, *The Trumpet Major*.

> It was of the most beautiful colour that the eye of an artist in beer could desire; full in body, yet brisk as a volcano; piquant, yet without a twang; luminous as an autumn sunset; free from streakiness of taste; but, finally, rather heady. The masses worshipped it, the minor gentry loved it more than wine, and by the most illustrious county families it was not despised. Anybody brought up for being drunk and disorderly in the streets of its natal borough, had only to prove that he was a stranger to the place and its liquor to be honourably dismissed by the magistrates, as one overtaken in a fault that no man could guard against who entered the town unawares.

Another nineteenth-century novelist, Elizabeth Gaskell, reveals that these strong brews, and others like them, were capable of being laid down for exceedingly long times. In one scene in Gaskell's novel *Wives and Daughters*, Squire Hamley has broached a cask of ale laid down at least twenty-one years earlier at the birth of his first-born son, Osborne, and invites the local physician, Mr Gibson, to try it in honour of his second-born son, Roger, who has been chosen to lead a prestigious scientific expedition to Africa.

> 'You must have a glass full. It's old ale, such as we don't brew now-a-days. It's as old as Osborne. We brewed it that autumn and we called it the young Squire's ale. I thought to have tapped it on his marriage but I don't know when that will come to pass, so we've tapped it now in Roger's honour.' The old Squire had evidently been enjoying the young Squire's ale to the verge of prudence. It was indeed, as he said, 'as strong as brandy', and Mr Gibson had to sip it very carefully as he ate his cold roast beef.

But great novelists did not just write about strong brews. Jane Austen, another giant of nineteenth-century literature, evidently knew and appreciated a drink more commonly associated with North America, and put that liking in the mouth of the eponymous heroine of *Emma*.

> 'I do remember it,' cried Emma; 'I perfectly remember it. Talking about spruce-beer. Oh! Yes – Mr Knightley and I both saying we liked it, and Mr Elton's seeming resolved to learn to like it too. I perfectly remember it. Stop; Mr Knightley was standing just here, was not he? I have an idea he was standing just here.'

So spruce beer was drunk in southern England at the time of the Napoleonic Wars. Of course, the more regular brews were ale and porter, and in novels, as in life, ale was frequently drunk mulled and spiced. Here's Charles Dickens, describing the arrival of Thomas Codlin, proprietor of a travelling Punch and Judy show, at the Jolly Sandboys Inn in *The Old Curiosity Shop*.

> ... said Mr Codlin, 'fetch me a pint of warm ale, and don't let nobody bring into the room even so much as a biscuit till the time arrives.' Nodding his approval of this decisive and manly course of procedure, the landlord retired to draw the beer, and presently returning with it, applied himself to warm the same in a small tin vessel shaped funnel-wise, for the convenience of sticking it far down in the fire and getting at the bright places. This was soon done, and he handed it over to Mr Codlin with that creamy froth upon the surface which is one of the happy circumstances attendant on mulled malt.

Instruments for mulling ale in a coal fire, looking a little like slippers made of copper, are still sometimes found in antique shops in more rural parts of England. One particular version of mulled ale was purl, hot beer flavoured originally with wormwood, later with ingredients as various as juniper, horseradish, ginger, sweet sedge and 'snake-root'. Here's Dickens in *The Old Curiosity Shop* again.

'Did you ever taste beer?'

'I had a sip of it once,' said the small servant.

'Here's a state of things!' cried Mr Swiveller, raising his eyes to the ceiling. 'She never tasted it – it can't be tasted in a sip!' ... Presently, he returned, followed by the boy from the public-house, who bore in one hand a plate of bread and beef, and in the other a great pot, filled with some very fragrant compound, which sent forth a grateful steam, and was indeed choice purl, made after a particular recipe which Mr Swiveller had imparted to the landlord, at a period when he was deep in his books and desirous to conciliate his friendship.

Much can be learnt about beer from Dickens, undoubtedly the beeriest of great novelists – for example, that it was entirely unremarkable to give boarding-school pupils as young as six years old table-beer to drink with their meals, as happened to Paul Dombey in *Dombey and Son*, where at Mr Bimber's school in Brighton 'it was darkly rumoured that the butler, regarding him with favour such as that stern man had never shown before to mortal boy, had sometimes mingled porter with his table-beer to make him strong'.

Dickens was the novelist of inns, taverns and pubs – the Maypole Inn in *Barnaby Rudge*, for example, is almost one of the main characters in the book – and he namechecks a number of well-known London brewers in his works. In *David Copperfield*, for example, Mrs Micawber tells David,

I have long felt the Brewing business to be particularly adapted to Mr Micawber. Look at Barclay and Perkins! Look at Truman, Hanbury, and Buxton! It is on that extensive footing that Mr Micawber, I know from my own knowledge of him, is calculated to shine; and the profits, I am told, are e-NOR-MOUS! But if Mr Micawber cannot get into those firms – which decline to answer his letters, when he offers his services even in an inferior capacity – what is the use of dwelling upon that idea? None.

The two firms who had refused to even answer Wilkins Micawber's letters were numbers one and two among the giant

London porter brewers for much of the nineteenth century. Dickens's great rival, William Makepeace Thackeray, names another London brewery, Hodgson's of Bow, pioneers of what became known as India Pale Ale, in one of his minor pieces, *The Tremendous Adventures of Major Gahagan*, set in India.

> ... old Jowler [the colonel of the regiment] was always happy to have my company at this meal; it amused him, he said, to see me drink Hodgson's pale ale (I drank two hundred and thirty-four dozen the first year I was in Bengal).

This reveals that it was the officers and gentlemen (and indeed, gentleladies) who drank Hodgson's, rather than the common soldiers. (We might suspect Thackeray of exaggerating for comedic effect in suggesting that Major Gahagan drank seven bottles of IPA a day, every day, but not necessarily.) Thackeray must have been a pale ale fan. In his best-known novel, *Vanity Fair*, the East India Company employee Jos Sedley (who would certainly have drunk his share of Hodgson's) is on his way from Southampton, where his ship has just landed, to London. 'At Alton he stepped out of the carriage at his servant's request and imbibed some of the ale for which the place is famous.' Alton, in Hampshire, had water very similar to that of Burton upon Trent, and supplied a fair portion of London with pale ales from two separate breweries. Until very recently it was still the home to one of Britain's largest lager breweries.

Not all the namechecks for brewers by novelists are as upfront as the ones by Dickens and Thackeray. Henry James, for example, in his novel *The American*, has his hero's French friend mortally shot in a duel by someone called Stanislas Kapp, 'the son and heir of a rich brewer of Strasbourg' who was 'making ducks and drakes of the paternal brewery' (that is, frittering away the family fortune). This is James having a rare joke with, or at, his readers: the biggest brewery in Strasbourg, later known as the Kronenbourg brewery, was actually owned by a family called Hatt, rather than Kapp. We see what you did there, Hank.

There are almost no works by great books' novelists about breweries, sadly. One of the few is *Rachel Ray*, by Anthony Trollope. The subplot features a brewery called Bungall and Tappit in the made-up Devon town of Baslehurst. Young Luke Rowan inherits a big slice of the brewery from his great-aunt Bungall, and comes to Baslehurst determined to improve its frankly second-rate product, against the opposition of the elderly Mr Tappit, who has run the brewery his way since Mr Bungall died and is perfectly happy making a profit from something not much better than vinegar. At one point, Luke is wandering the brewery feeling depressed at his inability to persuade the pretty Baslehurst lass Rachel Ray to marry him, and grumpy Baslehurst brewer Mr Tappit to lift his game: '"It would break my heart to be sending out such stuff as that all my life," he said to himself, as he watched the muddy stream run out of the shallow coolers. He had resolved that he would brew good beer.' This suggests Trollope had seen a brewery in operation, including the wide coolships, the technology used by brewers to bring down the temperature of their wort in the time before refrigeration.

Bungall's brewery is one of several similarly named brewing concerns that appear in Trollope's books. We can guess that Trollope and the little Trollopes played the card game Happy Families, which, in its Victorian version, included Mr Bung the Brewer; in another novel, *Mr Scarborough's Family*, Thoroughbung's brewery, Buntingford (a small town about 20 miles outside London) plays a minor role, while in *The Prime Minister*, one of Trollope's series of political novels, a brewer in the town of Silverbridge who narrowly misses becoming an MP is called Du Boung. One might feel that George Eliot is ranked a greater novelist than Trollope in part because of the way she gave Harry Toller, the Unitarian owner of the brewery in *Middlemarch* whose daughter marries Ned Plumdale, a much more likely sounding name.

The characters in the original Happy Families set were drawn by a young John Tenniel, who later became famous as a cartoonist for *Punch* magazine and as the original illustrator for *Alice in Wonderland*. Tenniel gave Mr Bung and his son Master Bung the red stocking cap, which, together with an apron, was effectively the brewer's uniform. He also gave them barrels for bodies, with Mr Bung's marked 'XXX' and Master Bung's 'XX'; Mrs Bung is advertising 'Dublin Stout', while Miss Bung is stylishly dressed, albeit with hatpins and a muff that both say 'XX'. The brewer's red cap gradually vanished, though at least one brewery, J. W. Green's in Luton, Bedfordshire, attempted to keep them going. In 1947 the *Luton News* was reporting that the brewers at the Luton brewery were wearing red-tasselled caps, which had been supplied by the company since the 1930s to encourage the old tradition, while the maltsters wore green ones. The J. W. Green Group annual convention programme for 1953 said,

> TRADITIONAL HEADGEAR. An interesting tradition at the Luton Brewery is that of the men in the brewing department wearing red stockinette caps whilst at work. The Luton Brewery has always been noted for this particular form of cap, which, of course, is the traditional brewer's headgear. Long after its use had ceased elsewhere, this link with the past survived at Luton, and there is no intention of dropping the custom. The Company's trade mark shows the old-time brewery employee wearing the brewery cap and carrying a green barrel.

(It was the habit of real Victorian happy families, incidentally, when they were sitting around on long winter evenings waiting for Alexander Logie Baird to be born and invent television, and they were tired of card games such as Happy Families, to read to each other from novels. Trollope apparently used to like slipping into his own works lines to trip up the *paterfamilias* as he read to his offspring, which is why you will find in the middle of *Phineas Redux*, another of his political fictions, the sentence, 'There's nothing like a good screw.' How true. A screw, of course, as you will know, is a broken-winded horse ...)

Several appearances of brewers in novels are as a plot device, a sort of *deus ex brasiaria*, some of whose vast wealth can be sprinkled over the hero or heroine to help them overcome all obstacles in the way of happiness. The gentry and the nobility had a distaste for trade but no distaste for the enormous wagonloads of money that ale and porter brought in, wealth that bought big brewers the key to polite society. As Herbert Pocket tells the hero, Pip, in Dickens's *Great Expectations*, 'I don't know why it should be a crack thing to be a brewer, but it is indisputable that while you cannot possibly be genteel and bake, you may be as genteel as never was and brew. You see it every day.'

Similarly, in Thackeray's novel *Pendennis*, Major Pendennis says to his nephew about Henry Foker, son of a porter brewer from Lambeth in London, 'I've no pride about me, Pen. I like a man of birth certainly, but dammy, I like a brewery which brings in a man fourteen thousand a year; hey.'

Thackeray, who liked to recycle his characters as much as Trollope liked to call brewers variations on Bung, had introduced Foker's brewery in an earlier work, *The Virginians*. This was set in the 1750s–70s, and is about two young brothers from a plantation-owning family and their adventures in America and England. One of the brothers is hauled out of married poverty in London by becoming a tutor to Mr Foker's son. The Virginian and the brewer become friends, and after the Virginian inherits a baronetcy and an estate in Essex, Warrington Manor, he writes in his memoirs, 'We brew our own, too, at Warrington Manor, but our good Mr Foker never fails to ship to Ipswich every year a couple of butts of his entire. His son is a young sprig of fashion, and has married an earl's daughter.' Thackeray based this last part on the London porter-brewer Samuel Whitbread, whose second wife was indeed an earl's daughter.

While the biggest London brewers mixed with the aristocracy, their brethren in country towns were not despised. When Ned Plymdale, whose father ran an extensive and profitable dye-works, becomes engaged to the daughter of the Unitarian brewer Harry Toller in *Middlemarch*, George Eliot has Ned's mother say,

> Sophy Toller is all I could desire in a daughter-in-law. Of course her father is able to do something handsome for her – that is only what would be expected with a brewery like his. And the

connection is everything we should desire. But that is not what I look at. She is such a very nice girl – no airs, no pretensions, though on a level with the first. I don't mean with the titled aristocracy. I see very little good in people aiming out of their own sphere. I mean that Sophy is equal to the best in the town, and she is contented with that.

The novelist George Meredith (who advised Thomas Hardy on his writing career) invented another London brewery, Cogglesby's, for his fourth novel, *Evan Harrington*. Old Tom Cogglesby, the bachelor co-owner, provides the cash that allows the young hero, born the son of a tailor, to finally win the hand of his fair Rose, daughter of a baronet of ancient family, who is also wooed by a peer.

The finest use of brewery as plot device, however, has to be in *Great Expectations*; how skilfully Dickens leads us up the brewhouse path, for while we are encouraged to believe, as Pip does, that his mysterious benefactor is the jilted and bitter Miss Havisham, the brewer's daughter, eventually we learn that … well, if you've never read the book, or seen the film or TV adaptations, I won't ruin it for you. Here instead is a description from the book of the rusty and verdigrigenous Havisham brewery in Kent, which had remained silent for decades after Miss Havisham was dumped by her fiancé on her wedding day.

No horses in the stable, no pigs in the sty, no malt in the storehouse, no smells of grains and beer in the copper or the vat. All the uses and scents of the brewery might have evaporated with its last reek of smoke. In a by-yard there was a wilderness of empty casks which had a certain sour remembrance of better days lingering about them. But it was too sour to be accepted as a sample of the beer that was gone.

A sad epitaph, for it also fits hundreds of other British breweries that have closed since the time of Dickens, even if they didn't all have an ageing loony in an increasingly ragged wedding dress haunting the premises.

15

In Praise of Rough Pubs

Around three-quarters of the way through the 1970s, I made regular trips to the north-west of England to see my then-girlfriend at Liverpool University. Occasionally we would visit Manchester, which could (and still can) boast a range of old-established family brewers superior to anywhere else in Britain.

Supported by a copy of the local Campaign for Real Ale guide, I would try to fit in beers in places owned by as many of these small operators as I could in a single trip. It meant visiting pubs for their proximity to each other, rather than the quality of the establishment/the beer. This is not always a good idea.

One day I found a place listed in the city centre that served the beers of a brewer from much further out that I hadn't then tried, and told my willing girlfriend we had to visit it. The outside of the pub looked as if the brewery estates department had last paid it any attention at least twenty years earlier; undeterred, we went in, got beers at the bar, sat down, and realised that the walls were covered in porn – not even the polite, airbrushed Penthouse/Playboy sort, but pages torn from magazines at the 'readers' wives' end of the spectrum.

Unsurprisingly, my girlfriend was the only female customer in the place, and every one of the customers looked like their only income was from acting as a copper's nark. There was probably a stripper on later. We didn't wait to find out. I might be alone here, but I find naked women too distracting when I'm drinking beer. Still, the experience gave me a marker for 'roughest pub I've ever been in'.

The Tidley Wink beer shop, a decidedly rough pub, from *The Drunkard's Children* by George Cruikshank, published in 1848. A Tiddlywink was nineteenth-century slang for an unlicensed beerhouse. (British Library)

I've found myself in a few actual strippers' pubs, and I've been in pubs where fights have exploded, though these generally looked perfectly respectable before it all kicked off. There was a bar in Glasgow where a table started brawling among themselves at half past five in the afternoon, for example: wonderful, I thought, someone's putting on the Glasgow pub experience for us without us having to stay out late and drink too much ourselves. The barman was given a fist in the face for going over and trying to calm it down, and I saw him later being given the classic folk-remedy of a raw steak applied to his blackening eye. Doubtless, this being Glasgow, the steak was later recycled onto someone's plate – well-done, I hope.

The only other place I've seen bar staff assaulted was in a pub in the back streets of Weymouth, normally a quiet seaside town with the nearest whiff of danger being the prison a couple of miles down the coast on Portland Bill. This time the barman had his shirt ripped off his back. As his attacker was carried out of the pub, the barman turned and glared at us; perhaps he felt we should have been more than spectators, or at least paid for our entertainment by offering to replace his shirt.

Rough pubs don't have to be a bad experience, of course. Around the same time as my visit to the Manchester porn pub, I used to travel out to a little rural beerhouse called the Goose, in the hamlet of Moor Green, part of the lost East Hertfordshire landscape of fields, woods and farms that seems 300 miles, rather than 30 miles, from London, and fifty years in the past.

The Goose, an isolated building of indeterminate age, had been selling beer for more than a century but was still about as close to being a private house as it could be while performing the functions of premises with a magistrates' on-licence. The pub sign was as rough as the pub: a painted sheet-metal goose, neck outstretched, perched on a 10-foot wooden post. There was no bar: the beer, brewed down the road by McMullen's of Hertford, appeared through a hatch in the wall of one of the two rooms open to the public.

The furniture was junk-shop, the gents' toilet was outside, and open to the sky; a luminous green fungus grew on the black walls of the urinals, looking as if it were about to release its spores and conquer the planet. The Goose was utterly basic and utterly marvellous, and the local Camra branch loved it, sticking it in the *Good Beer Guide* and travelling out regularly by the minibus-load to take on, and lose to, the cloth-capped locals at darts and dominoes. Even with Camra's help, though, the Goose could only have been doing minimal business, and it closed in around 1979.

There's still something special, though, about the pubs that are 180 degrees round the circle from chalkboard menus, gastro-food and four different house whites. Yes, the toilets probably whiff a bit, and the beer isn't that great, but who hasn't felt a thrill at being in a basic boozer at 3.30 in the afternoon with the racing on the telly high up the wall and only a Polish barmaid, a half-eaten packet of salt' n' vinegar and five or six other sad, silent losers for company, an experience that is as British as Trooping the Colour or the Last Night of the Proms ...

16

Give Peas a Chance

The jokes write themselves with this one, so I'm going to try to keep it as straight as possible; brewing with peas, strange as it sounds, is an ancient tradition, going back at least 400 years in Britain, and it still takes place in Lithuania, the United States and Japan.

The earliest mention I have found for peas in beer is from Gervase Markham's *The English Housewife*, published in London in 1615.

> Now for the brewing of the best March Beer, you shall allow to a Hogshead thereof a quarter [eight bushels] of the best Malt well ground, then you shall take a Peck [a quarter of a bushel] of Pease, half a peck of Wheat, and half a peck of Oats and grind them all very well together, and then mix them with your Malt ...

This, Markham said, would make 'a Hogshead of the best and a Hogshead of the second, and half a Hogshead of small beer, without any augmentation of Hops or Malt'. Even though the hop rate was just a pound a barrel, the strong beer, brewed in March or April, 'should (if it have right) have a whole year to ripen in', Markham said, and 'it will last two, three, or four years if it lye cool; and endure the drawing to the last drop'. That is probably more down to the strength of the beer – at some five and a half bushels of fermentables per barrel, the alcohol per volume was quite likely north of 11 per cent – than any magic the peas brought to the brew.

A few words about the word 'pea', incidentally: it began as 'pease', singular, with 'peasen' the plural. By the fifteenth century, 'pease' was often being used as both the singular and plural, and as a 'mass noun', like rice or malt. Eventually, by the seventeenth century, 'pease' was misanalysed as the plural of a singular 'pea'. 'Pease' and 'peasen' survive today only in 'pease pudding' and in place names such as Peasenhall in Suffolk.

The peas could be malted, and so could beans, vetch and even lupins, though Markham seems to have been talking about unmalted varieties, since he said elsewhere in *The English Housewife*,

> Now I do not deny, but there may be made malt of wheat, peas, lupins, vetches, and such like, yet it is with us of no retained custom, not is the drink simply drawn or extracted from those grains either wholesome or pleasant, but strong and fulsome; therefore I think it not fit to spend any time in treating of the same.

'Fulsome' was being used there in the sense of 'offensive'. Bitter vetch, *vicia ervilia*, is a legume with, as you've guessed from its name, bitter-tasting, lentil-like seeds, grown today for feeding to sheep or cattle and now only rarely consumed by humans. However, an informant called 'RT' from Derby, then one of the malting centres of England, was recorded in 1683 as saying,

> I have known pease and beans malted frequently, and many ale brewers desire some in their malted barley, because they make the liquor in working bear a better yeast, or barm, as here we call it; and certainly, being mixed in a good quantity with other malt, they make very strong liquor, which, as I am well informed, is apt to intoxicate and heat the stomach exceedingly.

Peas and beans, as Markham indicated, were not the only legumes made into ale or beer. Thomas Short, MD, writing in 1750 on 'malt liquors' (the catch-all for hopped beer and unhopped, or lightly hopped, ale in the eighteenth century) in a book with the lengthy title of *Discourses on Tea, Sugar, Milk, Made-wines, Spirits, Punch, Tobacco, &c, with Plain and Useful Rules for Gouty People*, said,

> Malt Liquors differ in respect of the Grain whereof they are made. Thus Pease, Beans, French Beans, Chick Pease &c afford a more tenacious, heavy Liquor, and such as requires a stronger Constitution to digest them, Wheat and Barley produce more nourishing and strengthening Liquors, seeing their Parts are more separable, and sooner reduced to a wholesome Spirit. Oats yield a more detersive kind of Drink, which is less viscid, has more earthy Parts, and a smaller Quantity of Oil in it.

Another writer in 1733 mentions malt made of 'Barley, Pease, Beans, Oats, Vetches, Buck-Wheat, or whatsoever else is cheapest'.

According to Richard Bradley, author of *The Country Housewife and Lady's Director*, published in 1732, 'Wheat-malt, Pea-malt, or these mix'd with Barley-malt, tho' they produce a high-colour'd Liquor, will keep many Years, and drink soft and smooth; but then they have the Mum-Flavour' – mum being the heavily herbed wheat beer originally made in Brunswick.

Four years later, William Ellis, in *The London and Country Brewer*, wrote, 'Some I have known put a Peck or more of Peas, and malt them with five Quarters of Barley, and they'll greatly mellow the Drink, and so will Beans; but they won't come so soon, nor mix so conveniently with the Malt, as the Pea will.' Ellis also recommended that when ageing 'Stout or Stale Beer', brewers should use an 'Artificial Lee' for the beer to feed on, and while some hung a bag of wheat flour in the cask for this purpose, '... some in the North will hang a Bag of the Flower of malted Oats, Wheat, Pease and Beans in the Vessels of Beer, as being a lighter and mellower Body than whole Wheat or its Flower, and more natural to the Liquor.' He gives a recipe for a hogshead of October Beer from Lichfield, in Staffordshire, which involves 'sixteen Bushels of Barley Malt, one of Wheat, one of Beans, one of Pease and one of Oat Malt, besides hanging a Bag of Flower taken out of the last four Malts in the Hogshead for the Drink to feed on', which must have been an unbelievable original gravity, at more than 13 bushels of malt and malted pulses to the barrel. (Allsopp's No. 1 Burton Ale, OG 1122, alcohol by volume 10.31 per cent, had only 4.5 bushels to the barrel.)

It wasn't only brewers who were making alcohol from peas and beans: distillers were, too, at least in Ireland. In 1758 the Irish parliament passed an Act 'to prevent the distilling of spirits from wheat, oats, bear, barley, malt, beans and pease or from any potatoes, meal, or flour of wheat, oats, bear, barley, malt beans or pease, for a limited time'. ('Bear' is bere, the coarse variety of barley still grown in Scotland.) Pea whiskey, anyone? Okay – in 1708 a book called *The Whole Art of Husbandry* said that 'out of one Bushel of Pease will come of Spirit at least two Gallons or more, which will be as strong as the strongest Anniseed-water usually sold in London', and explained how to make it.

> Let Pease be taken and steeped in as much water as will cover them, 'till they come and swell, and be order'd as Barley is for malting, only with this difference, that for this Work if they sprout twice as much as Barley doth for malting 'tis the better. The Pease thus sprouted, if beaten small, which is easily done, they being so tender, and put into a Vessel stopt with a Bung and Rag as usual, they will ferment, and after three or four Months, if distilled, will really perform what is promised.

In 1794 a book called *An Agricultural Dictionary consisting of Extracts from the most celebrated Authors and Papers* recommended 'pease malted after the manner of barley' as food for horses. But the references to peas, malted or otherwise, for brewing continue into the nineteenth century. In 1839 the author of *A statistical account of the British Empire*, talking about malting in Great Britain, said, 'Barley is the grain generally used, but oats, and other grain and pulse, viz beans and peas, are sometimes used for the purpose.'

Samuel Morewood's *Philosophical and statistical history of ...
the manufacture and use of inebriating liquors* in 1838 revealed
that 'owing to their fermentive properties', distillers 'frequently'
used 'the meal of peas beans and oats' in making their bub, a
mixture of meal and yeast with warm wort and water, used to
promote fermentation. Morewood also said that in Georgia,
bouza – a common word for fermented millet/grain-based drinks
across the Ottoman-influenced word, apparently from Turkish,
and not connected with the word 'booze' – was 'made from
peas, which is the common basis of it in that country'.

Even the pea pods were used to brew with in the United States.
A book called *Five Thousand Receipts In All the Useful and
Domestic Arts*, by Colin MacKenzie, published in Philadelphia
in 1825, declared, 'No production of this country abounds so
much with vegetable saccharine matter as the shells of peas. A
strong decoction of them so much in odour and taste an infusion
of malt, termed wort, as to deceive a brewer.' The book gave the
following recipe.

> *To make beer and ale from pea shells instead of malt*
> Fill a boiler with the green shells of peas; pour on water till it rises
> half an inch above the shells, and simmer for three hours, strain
> off the liquor and add a strong decoction of wood sage or hops, so
> as to render it pleasantly bitter; then ferment in the usual manner.
> By boiling a fresh quantity of shells in the decoction before it
> becomes cold, the liquor when fermented will be as strong as ale.

After 1839, however, references in Britain to peas being used in
brewing seem to vanish. It had been illegal for commercial brewers
in the United Kingdom to brew with anything other than malted
barley as their source of wort since the malt tax was introduced
in the time of William III at the end of the seventeenth century.
Suggestions for using peas, in the eighteenth century, therefore,
were aimed at the (still considerable) domestic brewing sector.
For whatever reason, however – I wouldn't wish to speculate –
pea beer looks to have nosedived in popularity in the UK from
the start of the nineteenth century.

It does not seem to have vanished elsewhere, however. In 1995 the beer writer Michael Jackson found beer brewed with peas being made in Lithuania. The Ragutis ('Drinking Horn') brewery in the city of Kaunas brewed a pale bronze lager called Širvenos, after the district in northern Lithuania famous for brewing Pea Beer, about 4.2 per cent abv, with 15 per cent or so of the grist being green peas. The brewery director told Jackson that the protein in the peas helped head retention, and that they created a 'thicker body' and 'richer flavour'. Ragutis is now called Volfas Engelman, and no longer brewing Pea Beer, I believe. But beer with peas in the grist is still, a reliable source (the Norwegian beer blogger Lars Marius Garshol) tells me, being made in Lithuania at the Biržai brewery in the city of Biržai, which is actually in Širvenos, Land of Pea Beer.

At least one small brewery in the UK, Nottingham Brewery, picked up the Pea Beer baton in the twenty-first century when it made a 'mushy pea' beer, a special for the 2001 Nottingham Camra Beer Festival. The beer was given the name 'Double Jeopardy', because if the beer didn't get you, 'the peas would'. The man behind the beer, Steve Westby, the beer festival's cellarman, said afterwards,

Philip Darby [the brewery's managing director] thought it would be a good idea if I came in and helped brew a special beer for the festival. I was keen to have a go but wanted the beer to be something a bit different. Now, there is nothing more that reflects the taste of Nottingham than mushy peas and mint sauce, which are traditionally sold at the annual Goose Fair each October. So I thought, why not brew a mushy pea beer? I put it to Philip and he thought it might work, although Niven [Balfour, head brewer], who undertakes much of the actual brewing work, had to be convinced.

'I went into the brewery to help with the brew one Sunday 11 days before the festival. We decided it should be a 4.2 per cent golden-coloured ale and it was to be brewed in the conventional way but with some mushy peas added in the mash, and, later, further peas added to the copper at the same time as the hops.

We used five boxes of peas on each occasion, they were not pre-soaked as we felt that the brewing process would achieve this. The brew went well except that the residue of the peas clogged up the filter on the copper and it took Niven about five hours to transfer the wort into the fermenter instead of the usual 20 minutes. If you wish to suggest to Niven that he should brew a further batch of the beer, be sure to be wearing a cricket box for your own safety!

Nottingham Brewery does not, indeed, appear to have repeated that experiment.

Today, Bear Republic Brewing in California makes an 'English Estate October Ale' it calls 'Clobberskull', with 10 per cent raw wheat and 10 per cent split peas, aged for 100 days in French-oak barrels to end up with a golden colour and an abv of 10 per cent, which actually might be fairly authentic for an eighteenth-century-style ale made in the household brewery at a country home like Downton Abbey.

The only other country, as far as I am aware, making beer from peas is Japan – and entirely because of that country's peculiar tax system than because of any heritage. Beer with less than 25 per cent malt is in a lower tax band, and Sapporo makes at least two beers, Draft One and Slims, using peas.

17

What Shakespeare Drank

An old friend of mine gained a PhD in the relative clauses of William Shakespeare, with particular emphasis on the later plays. Ground-breaking stuff, she told me, and I'm sure that's true. My own contribution to Shakespearian studies is rather less linguistic and more alcoholic; I seem to be the first person in centuries of scholarly study of the works of the Bard of Avon to point out that his plays clearly show Shakespeare was a fan of ale, but didn't much like beer.

To appreciate this you have to know that, even in the Jacobean era, ale, the original English unhopped fermented malt drink, was still regarded as different to, and separate from, beer, the hopped malt drink brought over from continental Europe at the beginning of the fifteenth century. It was made by different people; in 1574 there were fifty-eight ale breweries in London and thirty-two beer breweries, while Norwich had five 'comon alebrewers' and nine 'comon berebrewars' in 1564. In 1606 the town council of St Albans, 25 or so miles north of London, agreed to restrict the number of brewers in the town to four for beer and two for ale, to try to halt a continuing rise in the price of fuelwood.

This separation of fermented malt drinks in England into ale and beer continued right through to the eighteenth century, and can still be found in the nineteenth century, though by then the difference was that ale was regarded as less hopped than beer and, often, ale was light, beer dark. However, even in Shakespeare's time, brewers were starting to put hops into ale. In 1615, the year before Shakespeare died, Gervase Markham

"AN'T GET A QUIET PINT NOWADAYS WITHOUT A LOT OF HIGHBROWS SPOUTING POETRY AT YOU"

A view of Shakespeare down the pub by the Irish-born cartoonist George Morrow (1869–1955), from 1946, a time when a group called The Taverners was actually bringing performances of plays to pubs. (Author's collection)

published *The English Huswife*, a handbook that contains 'all the virtuous knowledges and actions both of the mind and body, which ought to be in any complete woman'. The book's recipe for strong March beer included a quarter of malt and 'a pound and a half of hops to one hogshead', which is not much hops by later standards, though Markham said that 'This March beer ... should (if it have right) lie a whole year to ripen: it will last two, three and four years if it lie cool and close, and endure the drawing to the last drop'. In his notes from brewing ale, Markham said, '... for the brewing of strong ale, because it is drink of no such long lasting as beer is, therefore you shall brew less quantity at a time thereof ... Now or the mashing and ordering of it in the mash vat, it will not differ anything from that of beer; as for hops, although some use [*sic*] not to put in any, yet the best brewers thereof will allow to fourteen gallons of ale a good espen [spoon?] full of hops, and no more.'

In the same book Markham wrote that 'the general use is by no means to put any hops into ale, making that the difference between it and beere ... but the wiser huswives do find an error in that opinion, and say the utter want of hops is the reason why ale lasteth so little a time, but either dyeth or soureth, and therefore they will to every barrel of the best ale allow halfe a pound of good hops.'

Markham was writing, however, in the middle of a battle fought for more than two centuries to try to keep ale free from hops. In 1471 the 'common ale brewers' of Norwich were forbidden from brewing 'nowther with hoppes nor gawle' (that is, gale or bog myrtle, a common pre-hop flavouring in beer, in Britain and on the continent). In 1483, the ale brewers of London were complaining to the mayor about 'sotill and crafty means of foreyns' (not necessarily 'foreigners' in the modern sense, but probably people not born in London and thus not freemen of London) who were 'bruing of ale within the said Citee' and who were 'occupying and puttyng of hoppes and other things in the ale, contrary to the good and holesome manner of bruying of ale of old tyme used.'

Almost sixty years later, in 1542, the physician and former Carthusian monk Andrew Boorde wrote a medical self-help book called *A Dyetary of Helth* which heavily promoted ale over beer. Boorde, who declared in his book, 'I do drinke ... no manner of beere made with hopes,' said that 'ale for an Englysshman is a naturall drynke', while beer was 'a naturall drynke for a Dutche man' (by which he meant Germans), but 'of late days ... much used in Englande to the detryment of many Englysshe men; specially it kylleth them the which be troubled with the colycke, and the stone, & the strangulion; for the drynke is a cold drynke; yet it doth make a man fat and doth inflate the bely, as it doth appear by the Dutche mens faces & belyes.'

A century on, another English writer, John Taylor, in *Ale Alevated into the Ale-titude*, 'A Learned Lecture in Praise of Ale', printed in 1651, agreed that 'beere is a Dutch Boorish Liquor, a thing not knowne in England till of late dayes, an Alien to our Nation till such time as Hops and Heresies came amongst us; it is a sawcy intruder into this Land.' Earlier, in 1642, a poet called Thomas Randall made the same point, in a poem called 'The High and Mighty Commendation of a Pot of Good Ale', that 'Beer is a stranger, a Dutch upstart come / Whose credit with us sometimes is but small / But in records of the Empire of Rome / The old Catholic drink is a pot of good ale.'

Shakespeare, being a far subtler writer than Boorde, Taylor or Randall, never made such obvious statements about his preferences. But he was a Warwickshire boy, country-bred, and he brought his country tastes with him to London. In 1630 a pamphleteer called John Grove wrote a piece called 'Wine, Ale, Beer and Tobacco Contending for Superiority', in which the three drinks declared,

Wine: I, generous wine, am for the Court.
Beer: The City calls for Beer.
Ale: But Ale, bonny Ale, like a lord of the soil, in the Country shall domineer.

Shakespeare's country-born preference for ale, and disdain for the city's beer, pops up across his plays. Autolycus, the 'snapper-up of unconsidered trifles', makes his appearance in *The Winter's Tale* singing,

The white sheet bleaching on the hedge,
With heigh! the sweet birds, O, how they sing!
Doth set my pugging tooth on edge,
For a quart of ale is a dish for a king.

By which he means that he can steal the sheet someone has left out to bleach in the sun, and exchange it for a quart of excellent ale in a nearby alehouse (which were, alas, sometimes places where stolen goods could easily be disposed of). But if ale is a dish fit for a king, small beer, according to Prince Hal – soon to be a king – in Shakespeare's *Henry IV*, is a 'poor creature', and he asks Poins, 'Doth it not show vilely in me to desire small beer?' Similarly, the malicious Iago, in *Othello*, declares that the perfect woman is fit to do nothing more than 'suckle fools and chronicle small beer'.

Nor was Shakespeare impressed by strong beer, judging by the fate of the villainous Thomas Horner, the armourer, in *Henry VI*, who is so drunk on sack, charneco (a wine from Portugal) and 'good double beer' (made by pouring the first mash back through the grain to extract more fermentable sugars), that his apprentice, Peter Thump, is easily able to overcome him and kill him in their duel.

Shakespeare's opinion of beer was so low, if we can assume that he was putting his own thoughts into the mouth of Hamlet, that he could think of nothing more depressing than being used after death to seal the bunghole in a cask of beer. Referring to the practice of using clay as a stopper in a barrel, the gloomy Dane tells his friend,

> To what base uses we may return, Horatio! Why may not imagination trace the noble dust of Alexander till he find it stopping a bunghole? ... follow him thither with modesty enough, and likelihood to lead it; as thus: Alexander died, Alexander was buried, Alexander returneth into dust; the dust is earth; of earth we make loam; and why of that loam (whereto he was converted) might they not stop a beer barrel?

In *Two Gentlemen of Verona*, however, Launce lists as one of the virtues of the woman that he loves the fact that 'she brews good ale', and tells Speed, 'And thereof comes the proverb, "Blessing of your heart, you brew good ale."' For Shakespeare, it appears, ale was fit for kings, and beer only for fools.

Centuries after his death, Shakespeare was adopted as a trademark by Flowers, the biggest brewer in his home town, Stratford-upon-Avon. (Flowers was founded, incidentally, by

Edward Fordham Flower, who had emigrated to the United States, aged thirteen, in 1818 with his brewer father, Richard. The Flowers settled in southern Illinois, near the Wabash river, on what later became the township of Albion – family legend says they turned down a site further north on the shore of Lake Michigan, believing it to be too marshy. Others were less fussy, and the city of Chicago was eventually founded there. Edward and Richard returned to England in 1824 and Edward began brewing in Stratford in 1831.) Fortunately, nobody ever pointed out to Flowers that Shakespeare wouldn't have liked the hoppy brew they were selling.

18

When the Vicar Brewed His Own Beer

Bing-drinking at the parsonage – no, that's not a typographical error. 'Bing-ale', according to *An Alphabet of Kenticisms* by Samuel Pegge, the eighteenth-century vicar of Godmersham, Kent, was 'the liquour which the fermor [farmer] of a parsonage [that is, the parson/farmer] gives to the fermours and to the servants, at two separate entertainments, servants first and masters afterwards, at the end of the year, when he has gathered their tythe'.

The 'tythe', or tithe, was the 10 per cent tax the Church of England was entitled to charge local farmers until it was abolished early in the last century. Undoubtedly the 'bing-ale' given to the farmers of the parish by the parson in return for their handing over their tithes was brewed at the parsonage, for this was still the age of domestic brewing. Almost every farm, many rectories, vicarages and parsonages, most stately homes and other country houses besides, from villa to cott, brewed ale and beer for family and servants. So, too, did university colleges, schools, hospitals and poorhouses. Until the very last decade of the eighteenth century, six in every ten pints of beer and ale drunk were brewed by private brewers. Only from 1790 did beer for sale creep above 50 per cent of consumption. Even in 1830, private brewers made one-fifth of all the country's beer.

Private brewing remained so common because beer was still the drink of choice for workers and servants, male and female. César de Saussure, a Swiss visitor to England in the 1720s, commented in a letter home that 'in this country ... beer ... is what everyone drinks when thirsty'. In 1800, the engineer

Bartholmey Rectory, where it was reckoned that the brewhouse was haunted by the ghost of Randle Crew. From *Barthomley: in Letters from a former Rector to his Eldest Son* by Edward Hinchcliffe, published 1856. (British Library)

Matthew Boulton calculated that his female servants required half a pint of ale (that is, a stronger brew) and a pint of beer with their midday meal and the same again at suppertime, while the men would need twice as much – six pints a day at mealtimes, two of ale and four of beer.

Among the champions of home-brewed beer was the Reverend Sir William Marriott Smith-Marriott, Bart, rector of Horsmonden in Kent until 1864. Sir William brewed at the rectory brewhouse, as his hop-farmer neighbours brewed on their farms, and according to Antony Cronk, in *A Wealden Rector*, 'In the Rector's opinion the stalwart character of the English Yeoman owed much to wholesome home-brewed beer. "Ah! would the humble peasant could / 'Ere taste a bev'rage half as good," he wrote, deploring the inferior liquid purveyed at the common ale-house.'

The best-recorded clerical brewer was Parson James
Woodforde of Weston Longville in Norfolk until his death in
1803, whose journal was published as *The Diary of a Country
Parson*. Woodforde regularly brewed strong and table beer, and
in 1790, for example, spent a total of £22 18s 6d on malt to
make beer: his butcher's bill, for comparison, was £46 5s 0d. In
a famous passage in April 1778, Woodforde wrote,

> Brewed a vessell of strong Beer today. My two large Piggs, by
> drinking some Beer grounds taking out of one of my Barrels
> today, got so amazingly drunk by it, that they were not able to
> stand and appeared like dead things almost, and so remained all
> night from dinner time today. I never saw Piggs so drunk in my
> life. I slit their ears for them without feeling.

Mentions of rectory and vicarage brewhouses are found across
the country. In 1745, an advertisement appeared for 'the
parsonage house of Brauncepeth' to be let,

> all new sashed, and in good repair, three miles from Durham,
> situate in a very pleasant sporting country ... with all manner
> of conveniences suitable for a nobleman or gentleman's seat,
> there being two coach-houses, a stalled stable for seven horses ...
> washhouse. brewhouse, barn, and granary room, together with a
> large fish-pond, sixty yards long, and fifty broad

which sounds more like a small lake than a pond.

At Berkeley in Gloucestershire a terrier (list of real estate) of
May 1682 described 'a Vicarage-house, with a Brew-house, and
an Orchard commonly called The Vicarage Close, containing
between three or four acres'. A 'true and perfect Terrier, shewing
all lands, houses, tithes, and other profits' belonging to the
vicarage of Wednesbury, in Staffordshire, in 1726 listed 'The
Vicarage House, consisting of 4 bays of building, being 2 stories
high, with a little study and a closet over it, the same at the west
end thereof, with one shiard [*sic*] and washouse [*sic*, again]
adjoining to the said house, and also one bay of building, called

the brewhouse, adjoining to the aforesaid house'. A terrier of the property belonging to the vicarage of Bradford in Yorkshire in 1820 included 'The vicarage-house, built with stone and covered with slate, sixty-four feet in length and thirty-one feet in breadth', and one 'brew house or out-kitchen adjoining to the same house eighteen feet long and ten and a half feet broad within the walls'.

One rectory brewhouse, at Bartholmey in Cheshire, was reckoned to be haunted. Edward Hinchliffe, son of the former rector of Bartholmey, writing in 1856, said that 'the restless ghost is said to be the spirit of "Randle Crewe"', and 'an old butler of my father's (still living,) solemnly asserts, that one night he heard the ghostly visitant knocking about the brewing vessels in the brew-house, and that he went to see what was the matter, but found no derangement of the tubs, &c.; all was perfectly quiet'.

At least one vicarage made its own cider. Lance Harman, who was later managing director of a brewery in Banbury, recalled that when his father was vicar at Old Cleeve, near Minehead in Somerset, before the First World War, the gardener, a man called Risdon, would make cider every autumn. Risdon's method was to heap the cider apples up under a medlar tree and, when they were thoroughly rotten, 'aided by all local birds and animals walking over the heap', they were shovelled into wheelbarrows and taken to the cider press, where they were pressed in straw. The apple juice was fermented in an open vessel before being barrelled for four weeks, after which it was considered fit to drink. One year 'there was what Father considered an excellent vintage': when the barrel was finished, a dead rat was found inside it.

Rectory brewing, and private brewing in general, was knocked on the head by William Gladstone with the so-called Free Mash Tun Act of 1880, which removed all tax on malt but taxed the beer instead. Now, if a private house was worth more than £15 a year, the occupier had to pay full duty on all the beer he brewed. In 1870 there were more than 100,000 householders, large and small, paying the then four shillings private brewing licence. After 1880 the number of licensed private brewers plunged precipitously, dropping more than 80 per cent to just over 17,000 by 1895. In 1907 that number had halved to just 8,605 'persons licensed as brewers not for sale'.

The memory of clerical brewing lives on, however, in two modern concerns. Rectory Ales was started by the Reverend Godfrey Broster, the Rector of Plumpton and a former Customs and Excise officer, at Streat Hill near Hassocks in Sussex, in 1995 and is still running today. Parson Woodforde, meanwhile, is remembered in Woodforde's Norfolk Ales, a small brewery begun in 1981 that is now one of the most successful in East Anglia.

19

What to Order in a Victorian Public House

If a twenty-first-century time-tripper stepped through the door into the public bar of a London pub in 1900, what would be the biggest surprise? Probably not the sawdust on the floor, or the lack of seating: most likely, I'd guess, the draught ginger beer on handpump.

The existence – and importance – of draught ginger beer in London pubs in the past is one of those uncountable little details of social history that slip past generally unrecorded because they seem so everyday and ordinary to contemporary observers that nobody bothers writing about them. Today's equivalent would be the bar gun – ubiquitous, observed by everybody who has ever stood at a bar to be served, and mentioned, I'll bet, in no account of the modern pub, anywhere. (It's the device used by bar staff to dispense draught cola, lemonade, tonic water and the like, looking like a shower hose with buttons on the top.)

Fortunately, back in the summer of Queen Victoria's last full year on the throne, one anonymous worker in the brewing industry spotted a reference in the *Daily Express* to 'half-and-half' as a beer mixture, a term not then used for several decades (it referred, in the early years of Victoria's reign and before, to a mixture of ale and porter), seized the nearest available umbrage at this anachronistic solecism and ran with it for 1,300 words of invaluable exposition on the drinks available from the pumps in a public bar in London, and how they were mixed together, which the *Express* printed for the education of future generations on page seven of its issue of Thursday 2 August

x

The public bar of the Olde Cheshire Cheese, Fleet
Street, London, pictured in 1899, where six handpumps
supplied thirsty printers and journalists with everything
from ginger beer to stout, from Old London Taverns by
Edward Callow. (British Library)

1900. And hurrah, digitisation and the web means that for a
small subscription to an internet site, more than a century later
we can read about what beer mixtures our great-grandfathers
drank without having to travel to the British Newspaper Library
in deepest Colindale, North London, and whirr through miles
of microfilm.

It's an absolutely fascinating piece, studded with gems – who
knew (not me), for example, that in a London 'boiled beef house'
(a restaurant specialising in serving 'a most delicious "portion" of
stewed beef done up in a sticky, coagulated, glutinous gravy of
surpassing richness', apparently), the accompanying drink of

choice was porter? Slow-stewed beef and porter: I'm channelling Harry Champion singing 'Boiled Beef and Carrots' just thinking about it.

It also confirms information from other sources, such as the availability of draught lager in at least some outlets in Victorian Britain, the identification of 'ale' and 'mild' as the same drink, and the higher status given to bitter, compared to ale and porter.

Here is the article in its entirety, with asides and notes (to be found at the end of this chapter) in square brackets by me.

Beers many and various and their mixture
By a member of 'The Allied Trades'

Recently in the *Express* a poet, calling himself 'The Impenitent', published some verses on 'My Pal', of whom he said: "Is blooming' drink is always 'arf-and-'arf.'

When 'The Impenitent' has called on members of 'The Trade' in London as long as I have he will have discovered that there is no such an article in Metropolitan Licensed Victuallerdom as 'Half-and-half'.

Were I Mr Lawson Walton[1], I should refer 'The Impenitent' back to a study of moral philosophy, just as that gentleman recommended it its study to Mr Balfour[2] recently. At any rate, the chapter on 'How we Classify', in Jevons's eightpenny *Science Primer on Logic*[3], would come in handy.

For in those portions of a public-house that cabmen frequent business is done on the 'Perpendicular System', ie, 'Stand up, order what you want in plain English, don't keep the *Express* after you have seen what you wanted to see, pay your money, drink up, and make room for other people.'

WHAT THE PUMPS YIELD
Now at certain houses you can get Lager Beer, drawn from a specially constructed tap, or you may buy 'Disher's Ten-Guinea Ale'[4], 'Bass's No. 1', 'Allsopp's Barley Wine'[5], and such like. But these are extras, and outside of ordinary trade. Usually in the 'Public Bar', otherwise known as the 'Four-ale Bar'[6], of a London

fully-licensed public-house, there are six liquids drawn from pumps, viz.:-

1. Ginger beer
2. Porter, called in London 'Beer'[7] and in the country unblushingly calling itself 'Stout'[8].
3. Ale, otherwise known as 'Four-ale', 'Cold Fourpenny', 'Mild', 'Mild Ale', &c. In Bristol it is known as 'Burton', but in many large towns, e.g. Nottingham, no malt liquor is sold at so low a price as $4d$ per pot (quart).
4. Bitter, called in bulk 'Pale Ale'[9] [sold for six pence a pot].
5. Stout[10].
6. Burton, strictly called 'Old Ale'[11] [sold for eight pence a pot].

Now we come to the combination of six articles taken two or more together. We now see how 'The Impenitent' has tripped in regard to his ''arf-and-'arf'.

A blend of all the above six articles should, properly speaking, be 'Waste', but there are ways and means of dealing with it, and treating it with egg-shells, and other finings, until it becomes again saleable as 'Porter'![12]

Don't fight shy of porter at a Brewery Tap, or at one of the famous Boiled Beef houses, or at any place you can trust. And this blending of malt liquors, which is so dear to the Londoner, is said to have given rise to the now meaningless word 'Entire'[13]. In days gone by, possibly, 'Entire Ales' gave a customer the flavour of a mixture though all drawn from one tap. The word now is a status of respectability, just as is 'Member of Tattersall's', another phrase with a past [a reference to the race horse auctioneers].

SOME BLENDS

Well a blend of one and two [ginger beer and porter] made 'Portergaff'; one and three [ginger beer and mild ale] 'Shandy' or 'Shandygaff'; one and four [ginger beer and bitter], 'Shandybitter'; two and four [the writer made an error and meant 'two and three', porter and ale] make 'Four-half'. It is a drink not so popular as is generally supposed. It is sold for the most part 'in your own jugs' at three-and-a-half pence per pot, though since the extra one shilling per barrel on beer in the present Budget [to help pay for the Second Boer War], a comparatively successful attempt has been made to get four pence per pot for four-half.

Porter is a halfpenny a pot [quart] cheaper. Two [porter] is not often blended with four [bitter] or five [the writer had erred again, and meant 'six', Burton] but with six [he meant 'five', stout] it makes 'Cooper', a drink rather out of favour. Three and four blended make 'Mild and Bitter'. Three [mild ale] and five [stout] are 'Stout and Mild'; it is never called 'Mild and Stout'; such a phrase would be barbarous. Three [mild ale] and six [Burton/Old ale] make 'Old Six' [because it cost six pence a pot]; it might be called 'Burton and Mild' but such a term is unusual. Four and five make 'Stout and Bitter', occasionally called 'Mother-in-law'[14]. Four and six are 'Bitter and Burton'; if you said 'Burton and Bitter', you would probably be served with 'Mild and Bitter', and it would serve you right.

The charge for Nos. 1, 2, or 3 is a penny per half-pint glass, a thick, almost unbreakable article, holding 5 per cent of froth at the top – a profit in itself[15] – and the successor of the old-fashioned pewter throughout nearly the whole of London. Four, five or six cost twice as much.

Blends at one and a half pence per half-pint are sold in a compartment known as a 'Six-ale Bar', or 'Private Bar', where there is a stool or two. In 'Saloon Bars'[16] nothing is under two pence per glass – there are a few houses where tankards are still obtainable, for the 'boom in public-houses'[17] is happily over and licensed victuallers have to think more about building up a business than they do of getting out of a business at an immediate thumping profit.

PROVINCIAL SPECIALTIES

There are numerous provincial variations of the various authorised terms. For instance, 'Beer' at an officers' mess means 'Bitter' – probably the only sort of malt-liquor kept[18]. But down at the Trent Bridge [cricket] Ground at Nottingham, 'Beer' means 'Ginger-beer'. Visitors to Nottingham should not fail to try 'Botanic', only don't let them put too much gin in it.

On the fringes of London there are numerous houses open for travellers during 'prohibited hours'[19]. These have made unto themselves a law that during these hours they sell nothing under sixpence a quart, and even during 'opening hours' they do not sell 'Four-ale' by itself at fourpence a quart. They foist off 'Four-Half' on the unwary. Of course, porter costs less per barrel than mild ale, so there is more profit by selling a quart of 'Four-Half' for fourpence than there is in parting with a quart of 'Four-Ale' for the same sum.

'Burton' does not all come from Burton-on-Trent. It should really be called 'Old Ale'. Some of the very best comes from Edinburgh[20]. Yarmouth, too, sends a lot to London. Indeed, there is a large firm of brewers which does not allow anything coming from Burton to be sold in the houses that are tied to them for 'Fine Ales and Black Malt'. This firm makes its own arrangements for supplying 'Bitter' from places other than Burton[21].

VIRTUES OF VARIOUS WATERS

'Fine Ales' means 'Four-Ale'. Water for brewing the very best 'Pale-Ale', ie 'Bitter', is the specialité of Burton-on-Trent. London water requires 'Burtonising' before it is suitable, but there is good water for the purpose in the immediate suburbs, while at Maidstone, Bishop Stortford, Nottingham, and innumerable other places, there are wells of excellent water for 'Pale-Ale' brewing.

Burton water does not come from the River Trent, but from very deep and extremely valuable wells of very hard water. Any sort of water does for brewing anything but the best 'Pale-Ale'. Home-brewed ale can still be obtained at Nottingham, but the big breweries are competing very hard against it[22]. At Birmingham the big breweries have nearly knocked home-brewed out of the field.

The 'Nut-brown Ale that was famed for its strength throughout the village of Grand Pré'[23] has its English equivalent at farmhouses in Suffolk. Trinity's 'Audit Ale'[24] does not come in everybody's way. But if you are a friend of the London managing director, and happen to be in the vicinity of Belvedere-road, Lambeth, just a little pint and a half jug all to oneself lets one know what 'Old Ale' should be like.[25]

1. Radical Liberal politician and MP.
2. Arthur Balfour, Conservative politician, Leader of the House of Commons in 1900 and later Prime Minister.
3. W. Stanley Jevons, FRS, Professor of Political Economy at University College, London.
4. A 1100OG strong ale, perhaps 10 per cent alcohol by volume, brewed at Robert Disher & Co's Edinburgh & Leith Brewery, Playhouse Close, Canongate, Edinburgh.
5. This must be the brewery's top-of-the-range Burton Ale, its equivalent to Bass No. 1 barley wine.
6. Because the biggest seller in the bar was the drink called Four-ale.
7. Porter was called a beer because it was well hopped: ales still had an idea of being less well hopped than beers.
8. A clue that as early as 1900 the idea of 'stout' as a strong beer was vanishing.
9. Another stake through the heart for those who insist that 'pale ale' and 'bitter' are different drinks.
10. Hand-pumped draught stout survived in Britain until at least the Second World War, though it was declining by then.
11. So, in Bristol if you ordered 'Burton' you got Mild Ale; in London if you ordered 'Burton' you got Old Ale. Same general style of drink, in fact, but the Bristolians were getting a weaker, younger version, the Londoners a stronger and longer-matured ale.
12. 'E's 'avin' a larf. However, such 'recycling' undoubtedly went on, with the 'waste' going into the Mild after draught Porter finally disappeared.
13. That was the story many believed: in fact, in the eighteenth century, 'Entire' was the standard term for any brew made from the complete run of mashes on one piece of 'goods', or malt.
14. The same joking nickname was also given to a mixture of Old and Bitter.
15. Clearly, calculated short measure has an ancient history.
16. The distinction between the 'public bar' and the 'saloon bar' in a pub has now effectively vanished, but for readers from outside the British Isles, and those too young to remember, the

'Saloon Bar' was the more upmarket room in a pub, where everything was slightly more expensive than in the Public Bar.

17. The period from about 1890 to 1899 when breweries rushed to buy up surviving free houses for fear that they would be locked out of the beer market if their rivals captured all the previously untied pubs.

18. From the first arrival of 'bitter beer' in the late 1830s/early 1840s to the early 1960s, the pale hoppy brew was the middle-class/officer-class drink of choice, while the 'lower orders' drank, first porter, and then mild ale.

19. 'Bona fide' travellers were entitled to a drink in a pub at any time, regardless of licensing hours. All you had to claim was that you had travelled at least three miles before you arrived at the pub.

20. This was the drink sold as 'Scotch Ale' or 'Edinburgh Ale'.

21. My suspicion is that the firm referred to was Courage, in Horsleydown, hard by the south side of Tower Bridge, originally an 'ale' brewer (that is, not a porter brewer, but a brewer of mild ale), which took pale ale supplies for its pubs from Flower's in Stratford-upon-Avon and then Fremlin's in Maidstone, Kent, before finally buying a pale ale brewery itself in Alton, Hampshire.

22. Nottingham had around 110 own-brew pubs in 1900, part of a then still enormous tradition of home-brew inns and beerhouses across much of the Midlands.

23. A quote from Henry Wadsworth Longfellow's epic poem *Evangeline*.

24. The very strong ale then still brewed at Trinity College, Cambridge for students and fellows.

25. A reference to the Lion Brewery Co. another of London's 'ale' breweries, which stood on the South Bank where the Royal Festival Hall now is. It looks as if Old Ale was a speciality. The 'South Bank Lion' at the east end of Westminster Bridge originally stood on top of the brewery before it was demolished in 1949.

20

The Brewery that Salami-Sliced Itself to Death

Late in the 1940s, Schlitz, the original 'beer that made Milwaukee famous', became the best-selling brew in the United States. The Wisconsin brewer wrestling the title from Budweiser, the self-styled 'King of Beers', brewed by Anheuser-Busch in St Louis, Missouri. The 1950s saw a continuous assault from Anheuser-Busch to win back the crown of America's favourite. The two brewers swapped the lead between them until 1957, when Budweiser went ahead permanently. The decisions taken by Schlitz's owners, the Uihlein family, to cope with their rival's dominance would eventually 'salami-slice' their company to death.

The brewery's roots were in a Milwaukee restaurant started by thirty-four-year-old August Krug, an immigrant from Bavaria, in 1848. Two years later Krug hired Joseph Schlitz, another German immigrant, from Mainz, to be his bookkeeper. When Krug died in 1856, Schlitz took over the management of the brewery, marrying Krug's widow, Anna, two years later and changing the name of the business to his own. The same year Krug's nephew, August Uihlein, began working for the brewery, aged sixteen. Over the next two decades, the brewery grew to be one of the two or three biggest in Milwaukee. Then in 1875 Schlitz was drowned after the ship in which he was travelling on a voyage back to Germany struck rocks off the Scilly Isles. Control of the brewery was inherited by August Uihlein and his three brothers, who had joined him in the business.

By 1967 the company's president and chairman was August Uihlein's grandson, the polo-playing, 6-feet-4-inches-tall Harvard

Schlitz drinkers around 1910, when the brand was still the beer that made Milwaukee famous, rather than the beer that made the perils of the 'salami slice' business strategy famous.

graduate Robert Uihlein junior, then aged fifty-one. Robert decided that if he could not sell more beer than Anheuser-Busch, he would at least make his company more profitable than his St Louis rival. The lagers that Schlitz, Anheuser-Busch, Miller and the other big American brewers made and sold in vast quantities took their name from the German word for 'store', since storing the beer for weeks to mature and improve in flavour before putting it on sale was an important part of the manufacturing process. The first step in Uihlein's plan to save money was a new brewing method Schlitz called 'accelerated batch fermentation', or ABF. This cut the brewing time for Schlitz beers from twenty-five to twenty-one days, and then to fifteen to twenty days, against the thirty-two to forty days of storage, or 'lagering', used for Budweiser.

The result was that Schlitz was now getting much more beer out of the same amount of plant, with all the boost in margins that meant. At the same time Uihlein instructed his brewers to begin cutting costs by using corn syrup to replace some of the malted barley used to make the beer, and by substituting fresh hops for cheaper hop pellets. The ingredient alterations were meant to be made incrementally, Uihlein's belief apparently being that drinkers would not notice each slight change to the product. Unfortunately, as commentators later pointed out, the steps from A to B and from B to C might have been tiny and unnoticeable, but the steps from A to M added up to a big leap.

At first, all seemed to be working. In 1973 Schlitz was able to boast that it had the most efficient breweries in the world, and was carrying out a rapid expansion of its production capacity. Its profits-to-sales ratio and its utilisation of its plant, in terms of capacity against actual production, were both substantially above the industry average. Market share was growing faster than at either of the other two big American brewers, Anheuser-Busch and Miller. Rivals tried to trip Schlitz up by claiming that its ABF brewing method meant it was selling 'green', or too-young, beer. Schlitz responded by changing the meaning of ABF from 'accelerated batch fermentation' to 'accurate balanced fermentation'.

Uihlein had already been given a warning about what could happen if drinkers felt a brewer was messing about with beer quality, however. In 1964 Schlitz had acquired the Primo brewery in Hawaii. By 1971 Primo accounted for 70 per cent of all beer sold in Hawaii. Then Schlitz stopped full brewing at the Primo plant, instead shipping dehydrated wort (the raw extract of malted grains boiled with hops) from its brewery in Los Angeles for fermentation in Hawaii. Islanders said the taste of their favourite beer had altered for the worse with this change, and Primo's market share dropped like a brick to just 20 per cent in 1975. Schlitz started full brewing in Hawaii again that year, but sales of Primo never recovered to their previous high.

Back on the mainland, Schlitz had attempted to respond to the growing success of Miller Lite, the first successful low-calorie beer, with the launch late in 1976 of Schlitz Light. But, perhaps because drinkers were already suspicious about what went into ordinary Schlitz, Schlitz Light was a failure in an otherwise expanding sector.

Meanwhile, Schlitz was running into trouble with its mainstream brand, after an attempt to disguise from consumers what it was putting into its beer. Because it aged its beer less than other brewers, Schlitz had to add silica gel to the product to prevent a haze forming when it was chilled. In 1976 the company began to worry that the US Food and Drug Administration would compel brewers to list all their ingredients on their bottles and cans. Its use of silica gel would show up in harsh contrast to its rivals such as Budweiser, who aged their beers longer, allowing the protein to settle out naturally, and did not need to use artificial anti-haze products. Anheuser-Busch was sure to point out Schlitz's use of an 'unnatural' product in its beers, and contrast this with the 'all-natural' Budweiser.

Schlitz decided to use another beer stabiliser instead, one that would be filtered out of the final product and thus would not have to be listed as among the ingredients. Unfortunately what Schlitz's brewing technicians did not know was that the new anti-haze agent, called Chill-garde, would react in the bottles and cans with the foam stabiliser they also used, to cause protein to settle out. At its best this protein looked liked tiny white flakes floating in the beer and at its worst it looked like mucus – 'snot', as one observer bluntly called it.

For months Schlitz kept quiet about the problem, with Uihlein arguing that the haze was not actually physically harmful to drinkers, and in any case not much of the beer would be kept at temperatures at which the haze would form. However, drinkers did complain, sales began to drop and Schlitz had to make a secret recall of 10 million bottles of beer, costing it $1.4 million.

Around the same time Robert Uihlein was diagnosed with leukaemia, dying just a few weeks later. An accountant, Eugene Peters, became the company's CEO and a geologist, Daniel McKeithan, who was the divorced husband of a big Schlitz shareholder, was appointed chairman.

All Schlitz's problems with its image, brought about by Robert Uihlein's tampering with the quality of the beer, were causing the company to start losing its second place in the American beer market to its Milwaukee rival, Miller. Even though Schlitz had increased its share of the US beer market from 7 per cent in 1950 to 14 per cent in 1977, Budweiser and Miller had grown faster. Peters and McKeithan pushed Schlitz's marketing department to go for a new 'high impact' advertising campaign featuring an aggressive-looking boxer who demanded, when asked to swap his Schlitz for another brand, 'You want to take away my gusto?' Instead of amusing viewers, the ad put them off: consumers found it 'menacing', and it became known as the 'drink Schlitz or I'll kill you' campaign.

By the end of 1977 Schlitz was on the slide, with profits, market shares and capacity utilisation dropping. Peters resigned after only 11 months, and was replaced by Frank Sellinger, the former brewmaster at Anheuser-Busch. Sellinger returned to traditional brewing methods and improved the product, but Schlitz was now operating in the red, and by 1980 its sales had been passed by another Milwaukee rival, Pabst, with a third Wisconsin brewer, Heileman, not far behind.

The end came quickly. In June 1981, Schlitz closed its Milwaukee plant to try to solve what was now an overcapacity problem. In October that year, Heileman made a takeover offer for the still-struggling Schlitz, only for Pabst to put in a rival bid. Both bids were vetoed by the US Justice Department on competition grounds, but in June 1982 the Justice Department allowed a $500 million bid by the Detroit brewer Stroh to go through. One analysis has estimated that the Schlitz brand lost more than 90 per cent of its value between 1974 and that final year of independence.

However, the debt Stroh took on to pay for acquiring Schlitz was ultimately too much for the Detroit company to carry, and it collapsed in 1999. Ironically, in the fire sale that followed, the Schlitz brand was acquired after all by Pabst.

The disastrous effect of deciding to reduce product quality salami slice by salami slice is now known in business circles as 'the Schlitz mistake'. It has been argued that Robert Uihlein's response to the increased competition from Anheuser-Busch and Miller, cutting costs to increase short-term profits, was a rational decision, and if there had been anything of a strategy of 'management of decline' about it, then the complete collapse in shareholder value of the late 1970s and early 1980s might have been avoided.

It would have been realistic for Uihlein to conclude in 1970 that the medium- to long-term future of the American brewing industry would be one where only two or three big companies would command the vast majority of sales: this is, after all, exactly what did happen, with, today, the Belgo-American-Brazilian giant Anheuser-Busch InBev and the South African-Canadian-American MillerCoors dominating the picture. It would also have been realistic for Uihlein to conclude that, whatever Schlitz's position was in 1970, there was no guarantee it would end up as one of those surviving two or three beer giants, and it was better to go for maximum profits while allowing the company to run down gently.

However, what Uihlein tried to do was have his brewery cake and eat it: cut costs, boost short-term profits and still maintain a long-term future for the company. The result was what the airline industry calls a 'controlled flight into terrain'. Cost-cutting cost the company its reputation, something almost impossible to repair for a consumer goods maker, and destroyed a concern that had once been the biggest in its field.

21

The Mystery of the Yard of Ale

You may have a similar mental picture to me of long-distance travel in Georgian times. The mail coach rattles through the arch into the straw-strewn innyard, chickens and geese flying out of the way, the outside passengers ducking to avoid losing their hats – or heads. The ostler and stable boys, alerted by the sound of the guard's horn as the coach came down the High Street, rush to unhitch the old, tired, sweat-spattered team of horses from the coach and lead them away for some hay and a rest, at the same time bringing out a fresh team. The red-faced landlord, in tan breeches, black waistcoat, white shirt and white apron, his hair tied back in a short ponytail by a black bow, hands up a yard-long glass brimful of ale to the overcoat-laden mail coach driver, who has no time in his schedule even to get down from his box. In a swing perfected by daily practice, the driver drains the long glass without a spill, hands it back down to the cheery publican and, refreshed, whips up his new horses, who

A footed ale-yard – these were highly unstable, which is doubtless why so few survive. (Author's collection)

gallop off back out onto the highway, the passenger-laden coach bouncing behind them and 10 more miles of muddy, rutted road ahead before they can all rest at the next stop. If there's not a painting of that scene on the oak-panelled walls of some pub dining room with eighteenth-century pretentions somewhere in England, I'll swallow the nearest tricorn hat.

It is a great tale, repeated often, and I never dissected it until I read the following passage a few years ago.

> The diarist John Evelyn (1620-1706) mentions a yard of ale being used to toast King James II, but the vessel has more plebeian origins. It was designed to meet the needs of stagecoach drivers who were in a rush to get to their final destinations. At intermediate steps the drivers would be handed ale in a yard glass through an inn window, the glass being of sufficient length for the driver to take it without leaving his coach.

This time, when I read about coach drivers and yards of ale, I finally went, '?'

I'm lucky, living in West London, a very short walk from a railway station. I can get up to the British Library at St Pancras in less than the 50 minutes advertised time between ordering books via the online catalogue and those books being brought up from the shelves. Turn right out of King's Cross past the stores built for Thomas Salt, brewer of Burton upon Trent, in the nineteenth century to keep shipments of pale ale in (now part of St Pancras International station), up the Euston Road and into the British Library, one of my favourite places on the planet (it even has a couple of hop plants growing up one wall). Check my coat in to the downstairs lockers, up the wide stairs, walk through the doors of the Humanities 1 reading room, find a seat among a couple of hundred or more other scholars researching who knows what, go up to the collection desk and pick up the haul: half a dozen or so Victorian and Edwardian books and periodicals.

There was certainly a fair amount of interest in the 'ale-yard' glass, though as H. Symer Cuming, who presented a paper on

'The Ale-Yard or Long Glass' to the British Archaeological Society in 1874, declared, 'The ale-yard and its parts form a singular group of vessels which are far more spoken about than written about.' Symer Cuming, who gave the capacity of a yard of ale as a quart, said he had 'searched in vain in printed books' for the history of the ale-yard, and I have searched in vain myself for any mention at all from earlier than my lifetime of stage coach drivers drinking from yards of ale.

Symer Cuming definitely doesn't mention stage coach drivers, though he gives a nod to the Alma beerhouse, near Galley Hill, Swanscombe, Kent, built in 1860, which in his era had a sign saying 'London Porter and Ales Sold by the Yard' (a joke also found at the George Inn, Bexley High Street, Kent, according to a writer in 1889, although see later). He mentions the mock 'corporation' at Hale, Cheshire (now in Trafford, Manchester), that had the 'Hale-yard' as its mace (another repeated joke: in Hanley, in the Potteries, the mock 'corporation' swore in each new member with a ceremony that involved drinking from a yard-long glass, though the contents were apparently port when the ceremony began in 1783, before changing to beer and, by the start of the twentieth century, champagne. Over the years the Hanley revellers broke their ale-yard at least twice). Symer Cuming also says that yard-of-ale glasses came in both footed and footless forms, the latter the familiar bulb-ended version. But of coachmen in a hurry not a word, though Symer Cuming was writing within twenty years of the last stage coaches being driven off the road by steam trains.

The magazine *Notes and Queries*, Victorian England's answer to Wikipedia, covered the subject of the yard-of-ale glass, or yard-of-beer glass, multiple times in the 1860s, 1870s and 1880s. One of the first mentions, in 1869, describes the ceremony of the 'long glass' at Eton, when 'RHBH' wrote,

> There still exists at Eton the custom of drinking a yard of ale, or, as it is called there, the long glass. Once a week, in the summer half, about twenty to thirty of the boys in the boats, or of the principal cricket or foot-ball players, invited by the captain of the

boats and the captain of the cricket eleven, assemble in a room at a small public house for luncheon. The luncheon, or 'cellar', as it is called, consists of bread and cheese, salads, beer and cider-cup. At the conclusion of the luncheon, a boy, previously invited for the purpose, is requested to step forward; he sits down on a chair, a napkin is tied round his neck, and the long glass filled with beer is presented to him. Watches are pulled out, and at a given signal he begins to drink. If he does it in good time he is greeted with loud applause; but if he leaves a drop at the bottom of the bowl it has to be refilled and he has to drink again. Two or three fellows are asked to drink at each cellar, and after this initiation they are entitled to be asked on future occasions. This is a very old institution.

These were schoolboys, of course, aged probably between fifteen or sixteen and eighteen. The 'beer bong' is not new. (A brief article in the *Lincolnshire Chronicle* in April 1899, incidentally, agrees that the Eton glass held a pint, indicates the 'long glass' ceremony still took place at that point and says the record time for emptying it was nine seconds.)

Another *Notes and Queries* correspondent, 'Ellcee', in 1869 said that for public houses, possession of, and flaunting, a 'yard of ale' glass was 'not at all an uncommon mode of inducing custom fifty or sixty years ago' – that is, around 1809 to 1819 – and a third pointed out that the South Kensington Museum (now the V&A) possessed what it called a 'forfeit glass' a yard long and with a bulb at one end, which was apparently made in Venice in the seventeenth century, and had been donated by the Duke of Bucchleuch. Others mentioned ale-yard glasses that could be seen at places such as Knole House in Sevenoaks, the Red Lion, Retford, a pub in Sandgate, Kent, the Wrestlers Inn, Cambridge and elsewhere. In 1882 a description was given of the custom associated with the yard of beer glass around Bexley, Kent.

In several houses may be seen an advertisement that 'Beer is sold by the yard.' And so it is, in accordance with a local custom.

There is a glass vessel exactly three feet in length, with a very narrow stem, slightly lipped at the mouth and a globular bowl at the bottom ... This is filled with beer, and any one who can drink it without spilling it may have it for nothing, but if he spills one drop he pays double. It looks so easy and it is so difficult, not to say impossible, to a novice. You take the vessel in both hands, apply the lip to your mouth and then gently tilt it. At first the beer flows quietly and slowly, and you think how admirably you are overcoming the difficulty. Suddenly, when the vessel is tilted a little, more the air rushes up the stem into the bowl and splashes about half a pint into your face. The cheapest plan is to treat the barman to a yard of beer and see how he does it. He will be only too happy to oblige you, and the Bexley ale vanishes with a rapidity only equalled by that of the beer consumed at Heidelberg among the students. The custom has extended far beyond Bexley and not only in the neighbouring villages but even near Oxford the yard of beer is advertised.'

(A later correspondent revealed that it was only, again, the George Inn, Bexley, that provided the yard of ale, and even it had stopped doing so 'within the last twelvemonth' when the glass was accidently smashed.) But again, not one writer talked of coach drivers in connection with yards of ale.

The same absence of evidence occurs in specialist books on drinking glasses. *The History of the Worshipful Company of Glass Sellers*, published in 1898, has a drawing of the Eton 'long glass', but no reference to coach drivers. *Beverages Past and Present* by Edward Randolph Emerson, published in 1908, calls the ale-yard 'decidedly original' to the English, describing it as 'a trumpet-shaped glass exactly a yard in length, the narrow end being closed, and expanded into a large ball.' Emerson gave a good account of the problems of drinking from a yard of ale.

Its internal capacity is a little more than a pint, and when filled with ale many a thirsty tyro has been challenged to empty it without taking it from his mouth. This is no easy task. So long as the tube contains fluid, it drains out smoothly, but when air reaches the bulb it displaces the liquor with a splash, startling the toper, and compelling him involuntarily to withdraw his mouth by the rush of the cold liquid over his face and dress.

Nowhere, however, does he mention coach drivers.

Emerson's claim as to the difficulty of draining a yard of ale is challenged by Percy H. Bate, author of *English Table Glass*, published in 1905, who describes ale-yards (and half-yards) as coming in two forms,

> those with feet and those without. Those without feet generally have a bulb at the base ... and this bulb is supposed to render the emptying of them at one draught very difficult, the ale leaving the bulb with a rush and drenching the drinker. But, so far as I know, the difficulty is more imaginary than real; at any rate I have not found it at all difficult to empty the only one I ever had in my possession.

Bate added, 'Being used as tests of skill at merry-makings and convivial assemblies, in which horse-play was not an unknown factor, most of the many that must have existed have been destroyed, and they are now distinctly rare.'

Among the vessels Bate mentions are footless 'travellers' glasses', which, he said, would be filled with spirits as the coach arrived at an inn for a change of horses, emptied by the passengers 'without delay', and 'the coach would roll on'. Apparently some inns would trick the passengers with glasses that, when filled with gin, looked of normal capacity, but which actually had extra-thick walls and contained much less than the tuppence-worth of spirits charged for. The whole operation was done so quickly that the coach was off out through the archway before the passengers realised they had been diddled. But on the coach drivers themselves, and how they might have been refreshed, he is again silent.

Specialist books on coach travel also fail to supply references to coach drivers and ale-yards. *Stage-Coach and Mail in Days of Yore* by Charles H. Harper, published in 1907, says the coach-horn was known as the 'yard of tin', but that is the closest it gets. However, in 1920 *The Connoisseur* magazine recorded that Mrs Bertha Challicom of Clevedon in Somerset, a collector of 'Nailsea' glass (the decorative pieces made by workers at the Nailsea glassworks near Bristol) had in her collection

> a 'Yard of Ale', inscribed 'Coach & Horses, 1820', and made by a Nailsea worker named Stevens, from whose descendants she bought it. This vessel ... was used for several years at a public-house known as the Coach and Horses (now the Smyth Arms), at Long Ashton, North Somerset, for handing up drink to the drivers of the old stage-coaches.

This sounds like a tale Mrs Challicom was told by the Stevens family: can we believe them, when they were talking about events up to a century earlier? Is the Coach and Horses yard of ale really something that was used to supply the driver with drink, or was it actually really a 'forfeit glass' used for drinking contests at the inn, which had the coach-driver story attached to it much later?

Whatever the truth, Mrs Challicom's glass is an isolated and rare mention of the coach-driver meme. The yard of ale continues to be mentioned as a curiosity through the first half of the twentieth century, along with the difficulty of drinking from it – 'Gardyloo!' a correspondent in the *Western Mail* wrote in March 1934 in a description of an ale-yard to be seen at Exeter museum – but still the coach driver makes no appearance in the story.

A book called *Rowland Hill and the Fight for the Penny Post*, published in 1940 and written by Henry Warburton Hill, talks about mail-coach drivers, and mentions the yard of ale, saying,

> The 'yard of ale' glasses were shaped very much like a coaching horn but have at the mouthpiece end a bulb rather larger than a tennis ball The glass contains a full pint. Considerable skill is required to drink the 'yard of ale at a draught'. The difficulty of emptying the vessel increases when nearing the end, as a slight

extra tilt may cause all the ale left in the bulb to fly into the face of the consumer. Much horseplay took place during the drinking: the glasses – which are now rare – being frequently smashed in the general jollification.

He does not mention them being used to supply coach drivers, however.

But the author does go into great detail over the sort of extra-thick 'traveller's glasses' Bate wrote about, describing another fraudulent use, this time involving the mail-coach drivers themselves.

'Joey' glasses were small glasses chiefly used for brandy. When filled, they present a normal appearance, the thick, heavy sides vanishing: when emptied, the fraud becomes apparent. Their name is derived from the 'Joeys', which were fourpenny pieces – so-called because Mr Joseph Hume, MP, caused these coins to be minted. The glass appears to hold fourpennorth of brandy. The mail coach driver not always wishing – or able – to take all the drinks offered him by the passengers, sometimes – after a wink at the tapster – was given what appeared to be a full glass, but actually was about half measure. With the 'joey', tuppence was surreptitiously returned to the driver. These glasses being almost indestructible are frequently to be found in a curio shop.

(Fourpenny pieces were actually older than Joseph Hume, who first became an MP in 1812, but he promoted their minting after they fell into disuse.) So – did mail-coach drivers actually prefer brandy to ale?

The earliest reference to the coach driver legend I have found after Mrs Challicom is from 1952, in a report of a day trip by the Devonshire Association for the Advancement of Science, Literature and Art.

On the return journey the party visited the ancient coaching inn at Hatherleigh [west Devon], this proving one of the most attractive features of the excursion, for the hostelry dates from 1450 ...

> To enter the rooms is to recapture the spirit of ancient times: for on the old walls are hung scores of objects of former use, powder-flasks, leathern bottles, mulling-slippers, and many other implements, particularly the 'yard of ale' and 'yard-and-a-half of ale' glasses handed to drivers of stage coaches.

(Mulling slippers, incidentally, are not what you put on your feet while wearing your thinking cap, but tin or copper slipper-shaped containers for filling with mulled beer and poking into the coals of a fire to warm the contents.)

The story was still not mainstream. The following year, 1953, the Whitbread brewery published a little book called *Word for Word: An Encyclopedia of Beer*, which said only of the yard of ale,

> Known also as a *long glass*, an old form or practical joke, companion of the puzzle jug of earlier centuries. Although the length varied, the yard of ale was approximately 3 feet long, shaped like a horn with a glass bulb at one end and open at the other. It held between 2 ¾ and 3 ½ pints and needed to be drained in one steady drink; if tilted too steeply, the beer ran out over the drinker's face.

Once again, stagecoach drivers fail to get a nod.

By the 1960s, however, barely a decade after the first mention of the tale, the 'yard of ale was a means of quenching a stagecoach driver's thirst at an inn stop so that he could remain in the box' story seems to have become mainstream, imitations were on sale, especially in the United States, claiming that yard-of-ale glasses were 'common back in the days of "merrie ol' England"' and were 'especially made to hand to stage *coach drivers* high up in their seat'. Any inn worth its fake-oak beams had a yard of ale on the wall as well. Here's a description from the *Brewing Review* of a 'pub' built as part of a British Week exhibition in Copenhagen in 1964 – read and weep.

> It was entirely built of wood with a false ceiling and a roof of realistic wooden tiles, and contained a collection of sporting

prints, a darts-board, a yard of ale glass, horse brasses and post horns and in every way typified the traditional 'local'.

Along with the yard-of-ale glass on the wall came the revival of the yard-of-ale drinking contest, so that pubs from Boston to Sydney had men drenching themselves in beer as they tried to emulate the Eton wet bobs and dry bobs of the nineteenth century and finish their yard in under ten seconds. (The current record is five seconds, apparently.)

But with all that, I hope you will agree, we have found no evidence that the yard of ale was originally 'designed to meet the needs of stagecoach drivers' in a hurry. In fact, there is no solid evidence that the yard of ale was ever used to refresh coach drivers at all (and if it had been, it certainly wouldn't have been handed up to the driver through an inn window, which would be an excellent way to either spill the ale or smash the glass). Instead, I think, it seems clear that the yard of ale was (1) produced as something of a show-off, for the glassmaker and the owner, and (2) primarily or almost solely supplied and bought as a 'forfeit glass', for use in drinking games and contests of skill, just as it is today. The 'used to refresh coachmen' story is just that, it appears – a story.

The Shadowy History of Sessionability

Brewers will tell you that designing a beer to have 'sessionability', the indefinable something which keeps bringing the drinker back throughout the evening to refill their glass from the same fount, is one of the most difficult problems they can set themselves.

Simple one-off tasting sessions are unlikely to tell you if you have achieved your goal: it's just like the 'Pepsi Challenge', where, in the battle of the colas, the sweeter drink wins in a head-to-head comparison, but over the distance the drier fluid wins. The only way to find out which new beers have sessionability, one brewer once told me, is to set a table up with a variety of free beers and ask the public to help themselves: the beer that is drunk the most, the beer that people come back to most often, will be the most sessionable.

I love session beers. I love the way they make a good evening down the pub with friends even better. What makes a good session beer is a combination of restraint, satisfaction and 'moreishness'. Like the ideal companions around a pub table, a great session beer will not dominate the occasion and demand attention; at the same time its contribution, while never obtrusive, will be welcome, satisfying and pleasurable – and yet, though each glass satisfies, like each story in the night's long craic, the best session beers will still leave you wishing for one more pint, to carry on the pleasure.

What is 'moreishness'? Like a great many qualities, defining it is hard, but you recognise it when you taste it. Strength doesn't have that much to do with it: that is, a weaker beer isn't automatically a session beer. Obviously if you're drinking large quantities it's easier if the beer is weaker, and the British traditions of drinking in pints and buying in rounds means that a session is unlikely to be less than five or six (British) pints – nine or so US 12-ounce glasses.

My impression is that Britons drink larger volumes than Americans, and for that reason the beer in the UK is weaker. The reason why Britain has recognised session beers and the US does not springs, I suspect, from the differences between British pub culture and American bar culture; in British pubs drinkers will stay all night long, and you want a beer you can drink all night long. I may be wrong, but American bars seem to be geared for shorter stays than British pubs. The requirement that a session beer shouldn't be too strong is secondary to the need for it to be a beer that can be drunk all night without the drinker tiring of it – 'quaffability'.

A good, quaffable session beer should have enough interest for drinkers to want another, but not so much going on that they are distracted from the primary purpose of a session, which is the enjoyment of good company in convivial surroundings. Like the chamber music that composers Mozart and Handel wrote for their patrons' soirees and divertimenti, a good session beer is a backgrounder to human interaction, capable of being appreciated as a work of art if you pause from conversation and consider it, but good-mannered enough not to intrude unless asked. A good session beer is a string quartet playing quietly, rather than *The Messiah*.

The 'session' itself, the long night drinking down the pub with mates, has, I think, always been a feature of British working-class life, even when beers were stronger. I'm sure that 'session beers', beers that were satisfying, moreish and not too obtrusive, existed even before high taxes bought in to pay for the war against the Kaiser – and kept on after his defeat – made it too expensive to sell beers at their pre-First World War strengths. The skill of British brewers was that they were able to carry on making tasty, satisfying, sessionable beers at lower gravities from the 1920s onwards.

The public evidently appreciated these lower-gravity beers, since they carried on drinking them, and when draught lagers arrived in the UK in the 1960s they were brewed at the same low gravities as the milds they were replacing, to fit in with the 'session' of five or six pints. Ideally, a session beer shouldn't be much more than four per cent alcohol by volume, simply to allow the drinker to wake up the next morning still able to remember how they got home.

The actual style of a session beer does not matter much: it shouldn't be too packed with flavour, too hoppy, too dry, too sharp or too sweet, because that will place the beer too much in the foreground. I've had sessions in German bierkellers with lager, and in Liverpool boozers with dark mild. A session is not about the beer; it's about the people, the conversation, the company. The beer, if it's a good session beer, makes the session flow, provides the salt. You'd enjoy the company without the beer, but the beer lifts it to a better, more satisfying level.

For me, bitters work best as session beers, because, I think, it's easier to hit that 'quaffability' target on the hoppy side of the circle than anywhere else. Among my top session beers – and this is very far from an exclusive list – are Timothy Taylor's Landlord, which once made me stay all night in a pub in St Albans simply because it was so good; Woodforde's Wherry bitter, which I have enjoyed enormously since I first tasted it at the Cambridge Beer Festival in the early 1980s and was struck at once by how good it was; London Pride, a delight almost everywhere I drink it; and another bitter local to me in West London, Twickenham Brewery's Naked Ladies, an excellent, balanced, hoppy 4.4 per cent abv brew (the beer's name commemorates a set of nineteenth-century marble statues of water nymphs, or, if Wikipedia is to be believed, Oceanids, in a council-owned public garden by the Thames. Twickenham people are very fond of the Naked Ladies, big-bottomed Victorian gels who look as if they would be very surprised if you pointed out to them that they didn't have any clothes on).

What do those four beers have in common? Three are in the 'best bitter' abv range and only one less than 4 per cent alcohol, none is backwards in the hops section, but all are very different in their flavours. Ultimately, though, any one of them would keep me in the pub with mates for much longer than a single pint.

Still, while the idea of having a session down the pub with mates is an ancient one in British culture, dating back probably to the Anglo-Saxon beer hall and beyond, when, and from where, did the term 'session beer' come into use? It's a surprising mystery. The battle against the Kaiser that saw taxes on beer soar also saw wartime restrictions on pub opening hours that remained unrepealed when hostilities ended. Instead of all-day opening, pub opening hours were now limited to two sessions, one at lunchtimes and one in the evening. Does 'session beer' come from the idea that it's a beer you can have right through one or other of these opening sessions? Strangely, the expressions 'lunchtime session' and 'evening session' themselves only seem to appear a couple of decades or more after the Defence of the Realm Act 1915 brought the concepts of a lunchtime and an evening session into existence, to try to cut alcohol consumption and keep munitions workers from spending all their wages down the pub.

The earliest reference to 'evening session' I have found is in, of all places, Samuel Beckett's first published novel, *Murphy*, published in 1938 and set in London, when one of the characters is trying to find a place to dump some unwanted material (I won't give the ending away by saying what that material is).

He was turning into the station, without having met any considerable receptacle for refuse, when a burst of music made him halt and turn. It was the pub across the way, opening for the evening session. The lights sprang up in the saloon, the doors burst open, the radio struck up. He crossed the street and stood on the threshold. The floor was palest ochre, the pin-tables shone like silver, the quoits board had a net, the stools the high rungs that he loved, the whiskey was in glass tanks, a slow cascando of pellucid yellows. A man brushed past him into the saloon, one of the millions that had been wanting a drink for the past two hours.

> Cooper followed slowly and sat down at the bar, for the first time in more than twenty years.

Lovely writing, and you don't have to know what *cascando* means to understand what it means. (Actually, it's Italian, and means something like a jumble – it appears to be one of Beckett's favourite words, since he used it as the title of both a poem and a radio play. 'The whiskey was in glass tanks' is a reference to the old pub practice of keeping spirits in a big glass container on the bar counter. Oh, and another snippet of social history – note that, this being the 1930s, the pub was playing the radio, not the television.)

'Lunchtime session' seems to turn up even later; I can't find any use of the expression before 1956, when Nicholas Montsarrat uses it in his 'African' novel *The Tribe that Lost its Head*, talking about the bar of the Gamate hotel in the made-up African country of Pharamaul, where 'the usual lunchtime session was in progress – both men and women, some drinking determinedly, some passing the time without urgency, some munching their sandwiches'. Those were all white men and women, it may be necessary to remind readers who didn't grow up in times when too much melanin in your skin could get you refused a drink even in an African country.

But does the phrase 'session beer' derive from lunchtime session/evening session? Some have claimed that it does indeed, because with only limited lunchtimes and evening 'sessions', British workmen would crowd in and drink as quickly as they could, which required lower-strength beer. But that makes the 'session' sound like the Australasian 'six o'clock swill', from the days when bars in Australia and New Zealand shut at 6 p.m. for the night. I don't buy the idea of workmen having to drink their beer as quickly as they could – the British, of course, buy their drink in rounds, each person in the 'round' taking it in turn to buy the group drinks, and they pace themselves as a group, so quick drinking is rude; it places an urgent obligation on someone to buy you your next drink when they may not be ready yet themselves for another one. Sessions, in any case, take place over several hours, which is why you want a low-strength beer – not because you're drinking lots in a short time but because you're drinking (cumulatively) lots in a long time. It's common to talk about having 'a session down the pub' or 'a session in the pub' with mates without that referring necessarily to being there all the time the place was open, and it seems to me more likely that this was the sort of 'session', with friends, that lent its name to a 'session beer', rather than the 'lunchtime session' and 'evening session'.

But what about 'session beer'? My personal recollection is that it wasn't a term-of-art found in the earliest days of the Campaign for Real Ale, and it only sprang up as a way of describing beers that could be drunk for a whole 'session' in the 1980s, at the earliest. Michael Jackson seems to have been the first person to use the phrase, in the 1982 edition of his *Pocket Guide to Beer*, though he was actually talking about beer brewed in Munich, referring to the 'everyday session beers' of the city, the Hell style of pale lager, which are typically 4.8 per cent abv, rather stronger than a British session beer would be. The term 'session beer' does not appear in Brian Glover's *Camra Dictionary of Beer*, published in 1985, but Jackson uses it again in the *New World Guide To Beer*, published in 1988, this time talking about what was then still Czechoslovakia, writing, 'The most commonly enjoyed beers are the 10-degree beers. At around 1040 [original gravity], with an alcohol content of 4 per cent by volume, these are what British brewers would term 'session' beers. These are consumed by the half-litre in Czechoslovakia's many taverns.'

It looks, from that, as if Jackson picked up the expression from talking to British brewers. As he was a hugely influential writer, once he started using the term it would have spread into more general use. All the same, the next uses of the term I have been able to find are both from 1991, one in Britain, when someone in the magazine of the Institute of Practitioners in Work Study, Organisation, and Methods wrote, 'A good tip is to pour it into a jug first, leaving the sediment in the bottle, thus enabling you to share the contents with your colleagues, which I would certainly commend, as this is definitely not a session beer,' and one from the United States, where Steve Johnson, in *On Tap: The Guide to US Brewpubs*, wrote, 'Session beer: Any beer of moderate to low alcoholic strength.'

Have we really, then, been talking about 'session beers' for only some thirty years, even though we've been drinking them for far longer? There's a debate to have the next time you're having a session down the pub with your mates.

23

Shades, Dives and Other Varieties of British Bar

When I lived in Hertfordshire, I was puzzled to discover that around the time Edward VII had ended his long wait to become king, there was a pub in the small market town of Baldock called the Pretty Shades. It seemed highly unlikely this was some sort of pre-First World War Tiffany-lamp-theme pub. So what was the origin of the name?

Years later I discovered that a 'shades' was originally the name given in the south of England to a basement bar. According to the book *Words, Facts, and Phrases; a Dictionary of Curious, Quaint, and Out-of-the-Way Matters* by Eliezer Edwards, published in 1882,

> The name originated at Brighton. In 1816 a Mr Savage, who had acquired the premises in Steine Lane formerly occupied by the Old Bank, converted them into a drinking and smoking shop. Mrs Fitzherbert [the Prince of Wales's mistress] at that time lived exactly opposite, and Savage was fearful of annoying her by placing any inscription in front of his house designating its new character. It struck him, however, that as Mrs Fitzherbert's house, which was south of his, was so tall as to prevent the sun from shining on his premises, he would adopt the word 'Shades', which he accordingly placed over the door where the word Bank had before appeared. The name took, and a large business was secured. Numbers of other publicans in London and elsewhere adopted the name Shades, which is now fully established in the language as a synonym for wine vaults.

The saloon bar of the Red Lion, off Piccadilly, London, in 1958, a place of pot plants on the bar and pork pies waiting to be sliced. (Author's collection)

I'm not sure I believe that, but the *Oxford English Dictionary* confirms that 'the Shades' was 'originally, a name for wine and beer vaults with a drinking-bar, either underground or sheltered from the sun by an arcade. Hence subsequently used, both in England and in the US, as a name for a retail liquor shop, or a drinking-bar attached to a hotel.'

John Badcock's *Slang: A Dictionary of the Turf, the Ring, the Chase, the Pit ...*, published 1823, revealed two establishments called The Shades in London. One was at London Bridge under Fishmongers' Hall ('Sound wine out of the wood reasonable and tolerably good are characteristics of this establishment'), while The Shades at Spring Gardens [presumably the Old Shades, Whitehall] 'is a subterranean ale shop'.

By 1949 Maurice Gorham could write, in *Back to the Local*, that 'Shades' was 'originally a generic term for cellars, now the name of one famous pub at Charing Cross [the Old Shades again] and of various London bars. When used for one bar in an ordinary pub, roughly equivalent to Dive'. So that explained half of the mystery. I'm still looking for a reason for the 'Pretty' part.

The 'shades' was just one of more than a dozen different types of bar that could be found in British pubs, besides the common public bar and saloon bar, many with careful, strict social gradations from one to the other, with a system of purdah and caste strict Hindus would appreciate; no woman would ever be found in the tap room, for example, nor any man coming straight from manual labour in the lounge or the public parlour, while only the landlord's intimates or regular customers would be served in the snug.

Maurice Gorham perfectly stated the situation as it still stood just after the Second World War.

> One of the most fascinating things about the pubs is the way they are carved up by interior partitions into the most unexpected and fantastic shapes. It is often quite startling to look up at the ceiling and realise that all these compartments, varying so widely in their geography and in their social significance, are merely sketched on the ground plan of a simple rectangular space. Pull down the partitions, and instead of a complicated series of bars you would just have a medium-sized room.

Today, of course – and the process was already beginning even in Gorham's time – those partitions have indeed come down. Now it is instructive to go into, for example, one of the big old boozers in the East End of London and imagine them not as they are, just one room, frequently, if they've been hipstered up, with unplastered brick walls and big, clear windows, but as they were fifty, sixty, eighty years ago, carved into three, four or more separate spaces by mahogany and etched glass barriers, each section with its own hermetic, exclusive group of customers who would rather walk into the wrong lavatory than the wrong bar, and served, often, by its own separate door to the streets outside.

In 1960 the *Times* brought out a book called *Beer In Britain* that featured a 'glossary of bars', dividing it into 'Southern Usage' and 'Northern Usage'. It was produced just in time: the social divisions that saw every man know his place, and know whether that place was in the public bar or the saloon, were crumbling. When I first started (illegally) drinking in pubs in the late 1960s, public bars and saloon bars were still, just, separate worlds, with the beer in the public bar, where the working man drank pints of mild, continuing to be 10 or even 20 per cent cheaper than the same beer in the saloon, where the working man's white-collared boss sipped at a half of bitter. By the end of the 1970s the price differentiation was disappearing, along with the social differentiation. Here's the *Times* guide to bars from the year Chubby Checker released 'The Twist' and Miles Davis recorded 'Sketches of Spain', when Harold Macmillan, prime minister of the UK, made his 'Winds of Change' speech in South Africa, and Senator John F. Kennedy won the American presidential election, with notes in square brackets by me.

SOUTHERN USAGE

Public Bar Where prices are lowest and furnishings simple.
Saloon Bar A saloon was originally a spacious reception room in a private mansion, then in an inn: applied circa 1835 to the better-furnished room of a public house. [But see later.]
Lounge Originally, the hotel residents' sitting room. Now a superior saloon bar, often with waiter service and with no sale of draught beer. According to Maurice Gorham in 1949, the Lounge, also known as the Saloon Lounge, 'is standard to the extent that many pubs have one, but it is a refinement on the Saloon Bar. It shows, therefore, that the pub possessing one has aspirations. It caters for a class of people who want something a little better even than the Saloon Bar. In pubs that have both, the

Lounge implies sitting at tables, having drinks fetched by waiters, and tipping'.]

Lounge Bar/Saloon Lounge Midway in status between the saloon and the lounge.

Private Bar Midway in status between public bar and saloon bar, intended for customers wishing to conduct private conversations, or for men accompanies by women: sometimes deputising for a Ladies' Bar.

Ladies' Bar Self-explanatory.

Bar Parlour An inner room, without a street entrance, reserved traditionally for regular customers or the landlord's inmates. Now rare.

Buffet Bar A refreshment bar (1869). Modern equivalents are the Lunch Bar and the Snack Bar, of saloon bar status. [I don't know where the *Times* gets that date of 1869 from; the earliest example of the phrase I have found is 1888. 'Of saloon bar status' means 'saloon bar prices charged'.]

Tap Room Originally (1807) a room where beer was tapped or drawn from a cask. Now an old-fashioned name for the public bar of an hotel or country ale house. Not found in London. [While 1807 is the earliest date in the *OED* for 'tap room', 'tap-room' occurs in a novel published in 1750 called *The life and adventures of Joe Thompson* by Edward Kimber, and must surely be older than that.]

Shades A basement bar. Rare.

Dive Originally an illegal drinking den located underground (United States, 1882), now usually a basement Snack Bar.

Cocktail Bar/American Bar Hotel bars now tending to spread out into public houses, sometimes taking over the place of the lounge under the name Cocktail Lounge.

NORTHERN USAGE

Bar, Public Bar As in the South.

Vaults Originally a cellar for storing food or liquor; now on the ground floor – equivalent to the public bar. (Vault in Lancashire.)

Smoke Room Northern and Midland equivalent of the saloon bar. There may be two: one for men only, the other for both sexes. [The one women were allowed in would actually be called the 'mixed smoke room'.]

Tap Room A public bar. Sometimes a room reserved for playing games, without counter service.

Lounge/Parlour/Public Parlour/Bar Parlour The best-furnished room. [In other words, 'saloon bar' was very much a Southern expression, according to *The Times*.]

Best Room/Best End Colloquial names for the lounge.

Snug/Snuggery Equivalent of the Southern bar parlour, but much more common. (Ireland only: one of a series of half-enclosed compartments within a bar.) Obsolescent. [I don't understand that last bit: if the snug was obsolete, how was it also common?]

News Room An old-fashioned name for the tap room, dating from the period when newspapers were supplied to customers. [There are, of course, pubs today that supply newspapers for customers to read, and an excellent idea too.]

Office Bar (Midlands) An inner room without counter service, equivalent to the Southern bar parlour, generally located behind the servery or the hotel office.

Buffet Bar North-Eastern variant of the saloon bar.

First Class/Second Class (Mens, Women's, Mixed) Variants of the saloon and public bars, peculiar to the Carlisle State Management System [This was one of the hangovers from the First World War, which had seen the breweries and pubs in and around Carlisle nationalised in an attempt to control drinking by workers at the armament factories in nearby Gretna – they were only denationalised in 1971.]

PUBLIC ROOMS OTHER THAN BARS

Jug and Bottle For the purchase of drinks for consumption 'off the premises'. Term now obsolescent. [Serving beer for takeaway in a jug was once common: my father used to be sent up to the pub, aged eleven, in the early 1930s in Willesden, North London to fetch his grandfather porter in a jug, strictly illegally,

because children weren't supposed to be served beer in an open
or unsealed container. Did he have a sly sip on the way home?
What do you think?]

Off-Licence/Off-Sales/Outdoor Department The modern equivalent.

The 'original' bar was the barrier in front of the buttery, the
storeroom where the butts (casks) of ale and wine were kept in
noble houses, monasteries and the like, which literally barred the
unauthorised from getting too close to the drink: those in charge
of the ale or wine stood one side of the bar and served it across
to either the drinkers or those who carried it to the drinkers.
In Shakespeare's *Twelfth Night* (1601), the servant Maria says
to Sir Andrew Aguecheek, 'I pray you, bring your hand to th'
Buttry barre, and let it drinke.'

Earlier than that, in around 1590, the author and playwright
Robert Greene (described by the *Oxford Dictionary of National
Biography* as 'England's first celebrity author') had written
in a book called *The Third and Last Part of Cony Catching,
With the New-Devised Knavish Art of Fool-taking* about a
trick practised by Elizabethan wide-boys, or 'cony catchers'
(cony as in rabbit, of course), that began with the cony catcher
chatting up two innocents in 'a common inn'. After gaining their
confidence he would order two cups of wine to drink with them
and then, on the pretence that he was going to 'step to the bar'
to get the inn-servant to add some rose-water to his own wine,
disappear out the front door with the cup, leaving the marks to
both pay for all the wine and explain to the innkeeper where the
other cup had gone. This is the first evidence we have that inns
had bars – at least, the sorts of bars that butteries had – where
people would be served.

Behind this kind of bar gradually developed the room that
became known as the bar parlour in the south of England,
the office bar in the Midlands and the snug in the North: the
landlord's office and storeroom, known at first simply as 'the
bar'. It was the innkeeper's private refuge, into which special
guests and friends might be invited for a drink. Charles Dickens,
in his novel *Barnaby Rudge*, described the looting of the Maypole

Inn (based on the King's Head in Chigwell, Essex) during the anti-Catholic Gordon Riots of 1780, where the landlord, John Willett, sits stunned while the rioters do their worst.

> Yes. Here was the bar – the bar that the boldest never entered without special invitation – the sanctuary, the mystery, the hallowed ground; here it was crammed with men. clubs, sticks, torches, pistols; filled with a deafening noise, oaths, shouts, screams, hootings; changed all at once into a bear-garden, a mad-house, an infernal temple; men darting in and out by door and window, smashing the glasses, turning the taps, drinking liquor out of china punchbowls, sitting astride casks, smoking private and personal pipes … wantonly wasting, breaking, pulling down and tearing up.

Gradually 'bar' spread in meaning to mean, in Britain, 'any room used for the serving of drink with a counter behind which stand the servers', and as larger establishments would have several of these rooms, serving different classes of customers, each type or grade of bar acquired a special name. But when did the names 'public bar' and 'saloon bar' arrive in Britain?

Earliest uses of the phrase 'public bar' are either legal, to do with 'pleading at the public bar' (not a desperate call to be served – although who hasn't made one of those? – but presenting one's case in a court or before a tribunal, either actual or metaphorical), or seemingly in the sense merely of 'a bar open to the public', which is how 'public bar' (more usually 'public bar-room') was used in the United States in the early nineteenth century.

The first use I have been able to find of the phrase apparently used in the 'modern' sense comes from a book called *The Itinerant, or Genuine Memoirs of an Actor* by Samuel W. Ryley [*sic*], published in 1808. 'One evening, in Manchester, we were in a public bar amongst a promiscuous company where C[ooke] [the actor George Frederick Cooke] was, as usual, the life of the party.' That's not definitely a use of the term 'public bar' in the modern sense of 'down-market section of a public house'; it could, again, just mean 'a bar open to the public'. But the passage is definitely (a) set in England and (b) describing something that probably took place between 1793 and 1800, since it mentions the prize-fighter Isaac Perrins, who moved to Manchester in 1793 to keep a pub, the Fire Engine, in what is now George Leigh Street, and who died in January 1801.

There is another example of the term from twelve or so years later, in a moralistic tract called *The Dialogists or the Circuit of Blanco Regis* by the pseudonymous 'Edward Meanwell'. This, the British Library says, was published '*circa* 1810?', but it must be *circa* 1821–1822, since it mentions George IV's coronation, which took place in 1821, and also gives 'Mr T. Dibdin' as manager of the Surrey Theatre; Dibdin was manager only between 1816 and 1822. Here, I think, we do seem to have 'public bar' in the modern sense, implicitly contrasting it with a more private or upmarket area to drink. 'You recollect poor Anne, that beautiful young woman of whom you was so much enamoured with; who, in open defiance and violation to common decency, called for a glass of gin at the public bar, in the presence of a crowd of persons.'

However, for the next thirty years or so the term seems to vanish, until it suddenly bursts into more regular use around 1856. *Glasgow and its Clubs* by John Strang, published that year, contains the passage, 'Champagne, hock, and hermitage, now so common, were found in few private cellars in the City, far less in the public bar of a tavern.' The same year, Dr Frederic Richard Lees wrote *An argument legal and historical for the legislative prohibition of the Liquor Trade*, complaining of apparently respectable drinking places filled with prostitutes, 'which can scarcely be said to come under the denomination of gin palaces, as they aim at enlisting under the banners of profligacy those who would (while sober) deem it beneath them to lounge at the public bar of a spirit shop'.

Three years later, in 1859, the report of a parliamentary inquiry into alleged corruption during an election in Huddersfield contained the following exchange. 'Now a word about having seen Jabez Wells at the Queen's [Hotel]; where was that was it in the bar?'

'In the public bar, I believe it was.'

That, I think, would pretty much underline that whatever had been going on before, by 1859 at the latest, 'public bar' was a recognised expression for a particular sort or grade of room on licensed premises, something confirmed by a description in the *London Society* magazine of January 1863 of the Angel, Islington, a famous coaching inn, long-vanished today and now remembered mostly for the Tube station and the square on the British version of the game of Monopoly named after it.

> The Angel Inn is certainly a most unangelic-looking place, reminding one of a dilapidated Mechanics' Institute, which has taken to beer in later life and broken out into innumerable 'bars' in consequence. There is the public bar full of "bus cads" and costermongers, the private bar with boozy tipplers from the street; there is the retail and bottle entrance with a narrow door, and there is the supplementary tap-room, which is apparently all window, and of which the chief characteristics are sawdust and spittoons.

(A 'bus cad' was the conductor of a horse-drawn omnibus.)

A report in the *Daily News* from Saturday 3 October 1874 described the 'great dram-shop' at the foot of the Trongate in Glasgow, and contrasts the public bar with the partitioned-off private areas:

> It is not easy to squeeze one's way into the throng of drinkers in the public bar, consisting of frowsy men, slatternly women, ragged stockingless, palid-faced [*sic*], preternaturally quick-eyed children. This, you see, is the public drinking, the *coram populo saturnalia* of those who care not who sees. Yonder, behind the wainscoted partitions, are the shut-in boxes, the drinking pens of Scotland, the private niches at the counter, where 'canny' folk sit and soak without being seen of men. These boxes are the haunts of 'respectable married women' who would on no account be seen drinking at the public bar.

For the comfort and guidance of strangers, the different bars advertised themselves on the outside in ways, of course, that still often survive today. An American description of London pubs in 1878 (*England from a Back Window*, by James Montgomery Bailey) said, 'They invariably have two, and in many cases three entrances; and are subdivided accordingly. These compartments are indicated on the glass of the doors; viz., public bar, private (or luncheon) bar and jug (or wholesale) bar.'

'Saloon' is an interesting word: it goes back thousands of years to Proto-Indo-European, where etymologists have deduced that there was probably a word beginning *sel-* that meant 'human settlement': the Russian for 'village' is still село, and the Lithuanian is *sala*. In Proto-Germanic the word seems to have shifted to mean 'hall': *Saal* is still a German word meaning 'hall'. Old English had *sele*, and *beór-sele* in Old English was 'beer hall' – or 'beer saloon', if you prefer. The word appears several times in *Beowulf*, the epic Old English poem about a hero's fight with a monster called Grendle and its aftermath, including the line '*Gebeotedon beore druncne oret-mecgas, ðæt hie in beor-sele bidan woldon Grendles guðe,*' that is, 'The sons of conflict, drunk on beer, promised they would wait in the beer-hall for Grendel's attack.' It amuses me somewhat to think of Ray Winstone (who played Beowulf in the film version of the story from 2007) having a drunken fight in a saloon bar with a monstrous opponent before ripping its arm off. 'Who's the daddy?' indeed.

However, *sele* dropped out of English, and 'saloon' comes to the language via Italian, which picked up the Germanic word for 'hall' and turned it into *sala*, 'hall', and then *salone*, 'large hall'. The French then took *salone* and made it *salon*, 'reception room', and from there 'salon' entered English as a word meaning originally 'a large and lofty apartment serving as one of the principal reception rooms in a palace or other great house', and then, more specifically, 'a room, more or less elegantly furnished, used for the reception of guests; a drawing-room'. By the 1720s, 'salon' was also being spelt 'saloon' in English, and by the 1740s 'saloon' was being used to mean 'a large apartment or hall, especially in a hotel or other place of public resort, adapted for assemblies, entertainments and exhibitions'.

Since drink – and food – would naturally be served in these saloons before, during or after the entertainments, it was equally natural that 'saloon' drifted semantically to take in the meaning 'a place where intoxicating liquors are sold and consumed; a drinking bar'. 'Saloon', in an American context to mean a place serving alcohol, looks to date from at least the early 1840s. In Britain, Charles Dickens was using 'saloon' to mean 'place where drink is served' in a letter to a friend in 1841.

All the same, 'saloon bar' is, in a British context and its British sense of the upmarket side of the pub, a little later than 'public bar'; the *Oxford English Dictionary* only found its first mention in 1902. Google Books lets us do rather better, but considering how ubiquitous the saloon bar was in British pubs in the twentieth century, finding the earliest reference to be only in the late 1880s is a surprise. Once again it's a teetotaller who is our helpful guide; those people just don't seem to be able to keep out of pubs. This is from an anonymously written book called *Tempted London: Young Men*, published in 1888.

> The most harmful class of taverns are those which are made the usual resort of women of bad character. We have had many of them pointed out to us, which derive the greater part of their trade from the business resulting from these frequenters. One tavern at Islington is one of the most notorious of this class. Here there is a large saloon bar which, after 8 o'clock at night, is almost monopolized by the class of persons just mentioned. They are allowed to remain there as long as ever they like, and no man is safe from their impertinences, if he once ventures into the saloon.

Undoubtedly, however, the expression had been in use for some time before it was recorded in print. The next year *The Builder* magazine recorded, in its issue of 9 November 1889, the results of a tender for 'new billiard room, approaches, alterations, and new staircase to concert rooms, extension of saloon bar and general decorations' at the Tufnell Park Hotel, North London, for Mr John Lees. The Tufnell Park Hotel was a rebuilding of the original Tufnell Park Arms (and was itself blown up by a German bomb in October 1940, to be replaced by the Tufnell Park Tavern). If the hotel's saloon bar was being extended, it sounds as if it must have been in existence when the premises were still the Tufnell Park Arms.

While no one, I am sure, can regret the ending of the social snobbery and sexism that made it necessary for most pubs to have a multiplicity of bars, I'm nostalgic for the multi-bar pub, despite what it represented. I love what happened to the Princess Louise in High Holborn, London, after it was taken over by the Yorkshire brewer Samuel Smith, around 2006. Sam restored it at some expense to just the way it would have been in the 1890s, complete with bar doors separating the open space into smaller drinking areas and snob screens, the rows of small centrally swivelling little opaque windows along the top of the bar at head height, found in the saloon bar or snug. The snob screens were closed when patrons in the saloon did not want to be seen by *hoi polloi* in the public bar or taproom, who might otherwise be able to watch across the behind-bar serving space their 'social superiors' drinking pints of pale ale. They could be opened, however, when it was time to attract the barmaid's attention to order another drink.

The refurbishment won the hearts of the Campaign for Real Ale's pub design awards judges in 2008, who gave the Princess Louise joint first prize, commenting that it 'reflects both its incarnation of over a century ago and the modern customer's wish to drink and chat in a cosy, quiet and private environment'. Drink and chat, chat and drink – I'm not sure which one I'd put first among pubby pleasures. But when the literal social barriers came down, and the pub became one large room, it made the chatting, against the background of everybody else's noise, a lot harder.

24

Words for Beer

There are four or five competing theories for the origin of the word 'beer' and, frankly, none of them are particularly convincing.

The same is true of the word 'ale', as it happens: despite 'ale' and its sisters, such as öl in Swedish and *alus* in Lithuanian, being found in languages from Britain to the Black Sea via the Baltic, no linguist has any good idea how it originated, with some of the ideas put forward being way out there in the unlikeliness ionosphere.

Of the four 'great' families of words meaning 'alcoholic drink made from malted grain', however, we can be reasonably certain about the origins of the other two, the Slavonic '*pivo*' group and what might be called the '*cerevisia*' group, after the Latin word for 'beer'. (Or, to be accurate, one of the Latin words for beer, since as well as the spelling we're familiar with in the scientific name of brewing yeast, *Saccharomyces cerevisiae*, the word also occurs in various Latin documents in the forms *cervisia*, *cervesia*, *cervese*, *cervesa* and *cervisa*.)

Taking this '*cerevisia*' group first, the Romans, who were wine drinkers rather than beer brewers, nicked their word for beer, in all its spellings, from speakers of a Celtic language. The original Proto-Celtic for 'beer' was probably something like **kormi* (that asterisk is the etymologist's symbol indicating a word that has not been attested, but whose form can be worked out on the basis of later variants), going back to an earlier Proto-Indo-European word **kerm-* (that dash means there was an ending

Sun Shines in the Hall: the dwarf Alvíss may be clever enough to know the words for ale and beer used by men, gods and giants, but Thor has outsmarted him and kept Alvíss around long enough for the sun to turn him to stone, thus freeing Thor's clearly happy daughter. Illustration by William Gershom Collingwood (1854–1932).

on *kerm* but we don't know what that ending was). *Kerm-* looks to be the root of a few other words in the Indo-European family, such as Russian *korm*, meaning 'fodder', an old Slavonic word *krma*, meaning 'nourishment' or 'food' and Latin *cremor*, meaning 'broth', or 'pap'.

In Gaulish, the Celtic language spoken in what is now France, the original *kormi* had become *curmi*, so the Romans must have borrowed the word for 'beer' from a bunch of Celts (perhaps the 'Cisalpine' ones, living on the Italian side of the Alps), whose accent had turned that *curmi* into *cermi*. What about the 'm' becoming 'v'? A general change shift in the 'm' sound to 'v' in the middle of words appears to be something that was happening, in British Celtic, at least, during or soon after the Roman occupation of Britain, so that, for example, the British kingdoms of Dumnonia and Demetia became, respectively, Devon and Dyfed (pronounced 'duvv-ed'). It looks like this m-to-v change was taking place in Continental Celtic earlier than that, perhaps some time between the Greek writer Posidonius, who lived from around 135 BC to 50 BC, and the Roman writer Gaius Plinius, better known today as Pliny, who lived from AD 23 to AD 79. Posidonius said the Celts of Southern Gaul drank a wheat-and-honey beer called *corma*, still with the 'm', while a century or so later Pliny gave the name of Gaulish beer in his *Historia Naturalis* (Natural History) as *cervesia*, now with the 'v', and with an added 's' as well.

It is from the form *cervisa* that French derived the word *cervoise*, still the term used in French for unhopped ale (and the origin of the French surname Leservoisier), while the Spanish and Portuguese look to have turned the *cervesa* version in Latin into *cerveza* and *cerveja* respectively. (In Galician, spoken in northern Spain, the word is *cervexa*, and it is still *cervesa* in Catalan.) The Spanish exported the word to the lands they conquered, so that, for example, in Tagalog (a language spoken in the Philippines, once part of the Spanish empire) the word for beer is *serbesa*.

In Britain, as on the continent, that change from m to v meant that the old Brythonic (British Celtic) word for 'beer', **korm*, altered its form, becoming **cwrf* (pronounced 'coorv') in old Welsh, then *cwrwf*, before losing the f to become modern Welsh *cwrw*, pronounced 'cooroo'. (Welsh being what is known technically as a 'mutating' language, incidentally, certain initial consonants change when nouns are used with prepositions, and that includes hard 'c', which becomes hard 'g': thus the essential order at the bar in grammatically correct Welsh would be '*Dau peint o gwrw ac baced crisps, plis.*' This is particularly important in the Lleyn peninsula, where you wouldn't want the locals to think you were from Swansea.)

Unlike Welsh, the sister Celtic languages Cornish and Breton kept the f/v after the change from 'm', so that 'beer' in Cornish is *coref*, and in Breton *coreff*. In the more distantly related Celtic language Irish, however, the word for beer stayed closer to the Proto-Celtic original, being *coirm*. By the time the Irish began settling in what was to become Scotland, though, in around AD 500, it looks as if the word *coirm* had dropped into disuse, since the modern Irish and Scots Gaelic for 'beer' is *lionn*, which originally just meant 'drink'. Coirm seems to have stayed on in Irish as a word meaning 'feast', however, just as an 'ale' in early modern English also meant a feast, as well as a drink.

(Incidentally, if you find anyone trying to assert that the word *cerevisia* comes from Ceres, the Roman goddess of agriculture, please give them a slap; this is perhaps the oldest beer myth in the world, going back at least as far as St Isidore of Seville (around AD 560–636), who wrote a book fourteen centuries ago called *Etymologiae*, which followed the usual Roman habit of treating all foreign languages as bastard forms of Latin and trying to find Latin roots for every foreign word.)

If you can order beer from Madrid to Manila with words derived originally from the Celtic, you can also go far with the Slavic *pivo*. It originally just meant 'beverage' in Old Common Slavonic, which itself inherited the word from the Proto-Indo-European base **po-/*pi-* 'drink': *piti* was the Old Slavonic for 'to drink'. Other words from the same root include 'potion', 'potable', the Greek *pinein*, 'to drink', and, indeed, 'beverage', via Latin *bibere*, 'to drink' (which we shall be coming back to). Today *pivo* or something almost identical is the easily recognised word for 'beer' across most of Eastern Europe and (thanks to the former Russian/Soviet empire) far into Central Asia: *pivo* itself in Slovene, Croatian, Serbian, Bosnian, Czech, Slovak, Macedonian, Ukrainian, Russian, Azerbaijani, Kyrgyz and Uzbek; *piwo* in Polish and Turkmen; and *piva* in Belorussian and Uighur.

In the middle of *pivo*land sits the curious case of Hungarian, a non-Indo-European language, unlike its neighbours, where the word for 'beer' is *sör*. An archaic and dialectical variant of *sör*, sometimes used informally, apparently, is *ser*. You might be tempted to guess that this comes from the *cerevisia* family.

Don't be. Guessing by untrained amateurs (in which category I definitely fall) will get real etymologists laughing, sneering and smashing eggs on your head.

As it happens, although there probably were Celtic tribes living in and/or near ancient Pannonia, the name for Hungary before the Magyars moved there (the Boii, for example, who gave their name to Bohemia), we can be pretty certain the local word for beer in Roman times was *camum*. A delegation from the Eastern Roman Empire to the court of Atilla in Pannonia in AD 448 found the locals handing out 'a drink of barley ... called *camum*', and *camum* was one of three types of beer (the other two being the Celtic *cervesia* and the Egyptian *zythum*) mentioned in the Roman Emperor Diocletian's lengthy *Edictum de Pretii* (Edict on Prices) in AD 301, an unsuccessful attempt to curb inflation by setting maximum prices on everything from a haircut to a pound of sausages.

In fact the best source for *sör* appears to be a word for 'beer' in Turkic languages, *sıra* (that's an 'i' without a dot there; *sıra* is pronounced approximately as 'sera' in the Doris Day song *Que sera, sera*). The ancestors of the modern Hungarians lived alongside Turkic-speaking peoples for around 400 years, up until they moved to the Danube lands shortly before AD 900 or so, and picked up quite a few words from them (including the word for 'word', apparently). At least two Turkic languages, Kazakh and Tatar, still use *sıra* for 'beer', though most others seem to have substituted versions of *pivo*, and Turkish uses *bira*, derived, obviously, from 'beer' itself.

Before we dive more fully into the tangled roots of the words 'ale' and 'beer', we have to tackle one particularly knotted strand first, caused by the curious fact that, four hundred years before English adopted the word *bier* from the Continent to describe a malt liquor flavoured with hops (altering the spelling to 'beere'), it already had a word, *beór*, that was used for an alcoholic drink. Around the time of the Norman invasion in the eleventh century, however, *beór* disappeared from the English language.

Most writers who touch the subject assert that *beór*, which is found much less frequently in old texts than the word that became 'ale' in modern English, *ealu* in West Saxon (or *alu* in Anglian), was merely a synonym for *ealu*. They take their cue from the *Oxford English Dictionary*, which said until very recently, under its definition of 'ale', that 'ale and beer seem originally to have been synonymous'. To back up this claim the *OED* quoted from a poem called the *Alvíssmál*, or 'Talk of Alvíss ', composed in the eleventh or twelfth centuries, probably in Iceland. This says (in Old Norse), 'öl heitir með mönnum, en með Ásum bjórr,' that is, '"ale" it is called among men, and among the gods "beer".'

But in fact this quote (which the *OED* appears to have nicked straight from Bosworth and Toller's Anglo-Saxon dictionary of 1882), although you'll see it repeated regularly when the history of ale and beer in Anglo-Saxon times is discussed, doesn't prove what the *OED* suggested it proves at all, that is, that öl and *bjórr* (*ealu* and *beór* in Old English) are synonyms, because the extract from the poem has been pulled totally out of context.

The *Alvíssmál* concerns a dwarf called Alvíss ('All-wise'), who, in Thor's absence, has apparently been given permission by the other gods to carry off Thor's daughter and marry her. Thor comes back and isn't over-happy when he discovers this, and (plot spoiler alert) cleverly delays Alvíss's departure by flattering the dwarf, telling Alvíss how wise he is, and asking him a series of questions about the names different beings, including men, gods, giants and elves, use for different items. This questioning delays the dwarf's departure with Thor's daughter until the sun rises, and, just as Thor had planned, Alvíss is turned to stone (which is, as you'll know, what happens when dwarfs are hit by the sun's rays), thus rather thoroughly stopping him making off with Thor's lovely young lass.

In the poem, the different words Alvíss gives to Thor are not meant to be exact equivalents. For the moon, to give one example, Alvíss says that the gods call it 'Flame', it is called 'The Wheel' in the house of Hell, 'The Gleamer' by the dwarfs and 'The Teller of Time' by the elves. These are all clearly poetic synonyms, not direct ones. When Thor asks Alvíss what the different beings call 'the seed that is sown by men', the dwarf replies that it is known as 'bygg' by men and 'barr' by the gods, bigg and bere in English, words for different types of barley, and not precise synonyms at all. In the final question, about öl, Alvíss says that as well as being known as *bjórr* by the Gods, some call it 'the Foaming', the giants call it 'the Feast-Draught', while 'in Hell they call it *mjöð*' – mead!

Now ale, made from grain, is certainly not the same as mead, made from honey, despite Alvíss saying that in Hell 'ale' is called 'mead'. No one, I think, is going to suggest that on the evidence from the *Alvíssmál*, 'ale' and 'mead' must have been originally synonymous. If these two are not synonyms, though used by Alvíss as if they were, we cannot assume that öl and *bjórr* were synonyms, either, even if Alvíss used them as if they were: the *Alvíssmál* is a poem, not a dictionary. Therefore the *Alvíssmál* cannot be used to argue, as the *OED* tries to, that *ealu* and *beór*, when first found in Old English, must have been synonyms for the same drink.

Having left that specific argument looking like the cat I once saw in the middle of an eight-lane highway in Abu Dhabi, let us drive on and examine evidence for Old English *beór* and Old English ealu being different drinks, and for what sort of a drink beór might have been. The late Christine Fell, Professor of Early English Studies at the University of Nottingham, fortunately for me, did all the hard work more than forty years ago, in a paper called 'Old English beór', published in Leeds Studies in English New Series Vol. VII, 1974. I've given the full cite there because, sadly, this isn't available via the internet, but if you can track down a copy (the British Library has one) it's fascinating.

(The *OED* section that covers 'ale' and 'beer' has recently been revised, and finally taken on board Professor Fell's arguments: the trouble appears to be that, as the Dictionary of National Biography puts it, when the *OED* was first put together the compilers of the *OED* were 'dependent on Toller's work for its pre-conquest references'. Toller had been brought in to complete Bosworth's work on a revised Anglo-Saxon Dictionary, after Bosworth died in 1876, and the section covering A and B was mostly Bosworth's doing. Bosworth seems to have been less of a scholar than Toller, and more likely to jump to conclusions: the entry in the Anglo-Saxon Dictionary for *beór* assumes without question that *beór* = 'beer'.)

To cut a long (twenty pages) study short, Professor Fell looked at the contexts in which speakers of Old English used the word *beór*, and what they used *beór* as the equivalent of in other languages. It is used to translate a passage in the Gospel of Luke, talking about Zacharias: in Latin *'vinum et siceram non bibet'*, which became in Old English *'He ne drinceÞ win ne beór'*. *Sicera*, and the Hebrew word it comes from, *shekhar*, to which we shall return, are translated today in the same Biblical passage as 'strong drink'. (I'm not going to translate *vinum* or *win* for you, I think you're smart enough to work out those for yourself.)

Elsewhere in Anglo-Saxon texts, *beór* is given as the equivalent of *ydromellum*, another word for mead, and it is also glossed as equivalent to *mulsum*, wine sweetened with honey. Both these drinks are likely to be stronger than *ealu*, a hint that *beór* may have been stronger than *ealu* too. The idea that *beór* was strong is reinforced by the instruction to pregnant women in one Old English leechdom, or medical tract, that they must not *beór drince* at all, nor drink anything else to excess.

To rub in the point that *ealu* and *beór* were seen as distinct and separate drinks a thousand years ago, Ælfric, abbot of Cerne Abbas in Dorset, who lived from around AD 955 to AD 1010, wrote of John the Baptist in one of his 'Homilies' that *'ne dranc he naðor ne win, ne beór, ne ealu, ne nan ðæra wætan ðe menn of druncniað'*, that is, 'nor drank he neither wine, nor *beór*, nor ale, nor any other liquor that makes men drunk.' Ælfric, who was a conscientious writer, clearly felt he needed to differentiate *beór* from *ealu*, as well as *ealu* from *win*. *Beór*, then, comes through from Anglo-Saxon texts as strong and sweet, and different to, or separate, from *ealu*.

There is also the Irish evidence. In the Irish version of the legend of heather ale, the drink whose secret recipe is known only to a father and son is called *bheóir Lochlannach*, *Lochlann* being the Irish for Viking. *Bheóir Lochlannach* is always translated today as 'Viking beer'. However, the word *beóir* must come from the Old Norse word *bjórr*. If *bjórr* was the same as öl, as the *OED* wants us to accept, why did the Irish feel the need to borrow *bjórr* to use for the heather brew, instead of using their own language's equivalents of öl, which were *cuirm* or, later, *lionn*? Why was this *bheóir Lochlannach* and not *chuirm Lochlannach* or *lionn Lochlannach*?

Professor Fell put forward a very good argument for *beór* in Old English (and its equivalent in Old Norse, *bjórr*) being a strongly alcoholic, sweet, honey-and-fruit drink consumed from tiny cups only an inch or so high: such cups have been found in pagan Anglo-Saxon graves from the sixth and seventh centuries AD. It is possible – indeed, I'd say somewhere between possible and probable – that *beór* was, in fact, fermented apple juice. The Anglo-Saxons cultivated apples, and it seems unlikely they would not have known how to make an alcoholic drink out of them: ripe apples will practically ferment by themselves. There is, however, no known Old English word that definitely means 'cider' – but at more or less the same time that *sidre*, the word that became 'cider', enters the English language, in the middle of the eleventh century, the word *beór* disappears.

That is far from conclusive evidence that the French *sidre* was brought over by the French-speaking Normans (and Bretons) who settled here after William the Conqueror conquered, and replaced the Old English word *beór*. It could be just coincidence that one word vanished as the other arrived. Curiously, in Normandy itself, which, of course, takes its name from the Old Norse speakers who settled there and later switched to speaking French, the dialect word for cider is *bère*.

Sidre/cider comes, via French, Latin and Greek, from the Hebrew *shekhar*. *Shekhar* properly means 'any strong alcoholic drink' (apparently from *shakar*, to drink heavily: the Yiddish for 'to be drunk' is *shiker*). What sort of drink Hebrew *shekhar* was, apart from, presumably, strong, we don't know (although in Akkadian, the related Semitic language spoken in Babylon 4,000 years ago, the equivalent word, šikarum, translated Sumerian *KAŠ*, beer: but in the Quran the equivalent word in Arabic, *sokara*, is used to mean any intoxicant).

In the time of St Isidore of Seville, who was writing in the late 6th and early 7th centuries AD, *sicera* was '*omnis potio quae extra vinum inebriare potest*', 'all inebriating drinks apart from wine', which included those made from *frumentum* (grain) and *poma* (apples), the saint said. Did Anglo-Saxon writers such as Ælfric know that Isidore's definition of *sicera* included it being made from *poma* and decide that because *beór* was made from *poma* too, then beór was the best translation of *sicera*? This is probably a speculation too far. There is no hard evidence that *beór* was made from apples and meant cider, and that this influenced in any way the translation of *shekhar/sicera* into Old English as beór. But I like to think it possible that Ælfric, who came, after all, from a cider-making part of England, included cider, as *beór*, in his list of drinks that John the Baptist eschewed, alongside wine and ale, just in case any of the Cerne monks thought it was OK to go whacking into the scrumpy.

Whatever the truth, it still leaves the actual origins of the words 'ale' and 'beer' as a surprisingly tangled mystery, with no particularly obvious root for either word.

Nor has anyone ever explained convincingly why the 'continental' branch of West Germanic (the one that eventually became German in all its dialects, and Dutch and Friesian) dropped the *al-* word for 'beer' it had derived from a supposed Germanic root **aluþ-* (that *, remember, indicates a word for which there is no direct evidence, but which has been reconstructed from later forms), and took up the word *bier* instead, while the 'off-shore' branch of West Germanic, the ancestor of modern English, together with the North Germanic languages (Norwegian, Swedish, Danish and so on) stayed with words derived from **aluþ-* – 'ale' in modern English, Swedish and Icelandic öl and Danish and Norwegian øl.

Let's look at 'ale' first, the word that originally, in English, meant an unhopped fermented malt drink. It's a word found across Northern and Eastern Europe; as well as in the Scandinavian languages, it occurs in the Baltic languages Lithuanian (*alùs*) and Latvian (*alus*), the Finno-Ugric languages Finnish (*olut*) and Estonian (*olu*) and the Slav languages Slovene (*ôl*) and Serbo-

Croat (*olovina*, which means 'yeast, dregs', I believe). There is no evidence that the Baltic languages borrowed the 'ale' word from the Germanic languages, or vice versa.

The word also appears away over in the Caucasus, in Georgian (apart from Finnish and Estonian the only non-Indo-European example) as *ludi* or, in a couple of mountain dialects, *aludi*, and in Georgian's neighbour, the Iranic language Ossetian, as *aeluton*. Georgian linguists believe their language took the word *ludi* from the Ossetians, who are the descendants of the Alans.

The Alans ranged from their original home near the Sea of Azov, north of the Black Sea, as far west as France in the late fourth, fifth and sixth century AD, down into Spain and along the North African cost to modern Tunisia, as allies of other invaders of the Roman world such as the Germanic-speaking Vandals and Goths. After the final defeat of the Vandal–Alan kingdom in North Africa in 534, some of the Alans look to have returned to the border of the Roman Empire with Persia as cavalry in the Roman army. It seems more than possible they picked up the 'ale' word from one of the Germanic peoples and brought it back to the Eastern Black Sea, where they met up with other stay-at-home Alans who had been pushed up into the Caucasus by the advancing Huns.

But where does 'ale' come from as a word? One school wants to trace it to an Indo-European base **alu-* (*-d*, *-t*), meaning 'bitter', a root found in the modern English word 'alum', the highly astringent salt used in, for example, leather tanning, and in the Proto-Slavonic root **el-uku*, 'bitter', which has apparently given words such as the dialectic Polish *ilki*, 'bitter' and the Czech *žluknouti*, 'turn rancid'. This would make 'ale' etymologically 'the bitter drink'. Unfortunately there is no evidence ale *was* originally a bitter drink: without hops and herbs (and English ale, at least, seems to have been drunk quite often without herbs) it would probably have been a sweetish drink to begin with, and then acidic or sharp, rather than bitter, as it aged and soured. Indeed, in a list of words in one now-extinct Baltic language, Old Prussian, compiled by a German writer in the fourteenth century, *alu* is glossed as meaning 'mead', fermented honey, which is definitely sweet, not bitter. So, no cigar for that idea.

The Indo-European expert Calvert Watkins of Harvard University suggests another possibility, that the Germanic root *aluþ- is related to the Greek *aluein* or *alussein* and the Latvian *aluót*, both meaning 'to be distraught', with cognates having to do with sorcery (Runic *alu*, 'a spell', Hittite *alwanzatar*, 'withcraft, sorcery, spell, hex'), and also 'hallucinate'. All these words in a variety of Indo-European languages do suggest that there was a Proto-Indo-European root *alu* meaning 'a spell'. The semantic link would be that after drinking *aluþ- the bewitched drinker would stagger about in a distraught state and begin to have visions. It's an interesting suggestion, but not a convincing one, for me; you don't automatically become distraught and start hallucinating once you begin drinking ale.

One minority group wants to link 'ale' with words in Uralic languages meaning 'tree sap', such as ālos or āllus in Sami, the language of the Lapp people, *ol* in the language of the Mansi of West Siberia and *yllu* in the language of their neighbours to the east, the Selkup. This appeals to me; fermented birch sap is still drunk in, for example, Belarus, Latvia and Lithuania (where it is called *kveisas*, surely linked to *kvass*, the Russian bread-beer, the name of which is reckoned to be descended from another putative Indo-European word for 'fermented substance', *kuath-so-*, also found in a Gothic word meaning 'foam up' and the Sanskrit *kváthati*, 'boil'). It is easy to believe the Indo-European peoples who later lived in Northern Europe nicked the idea of fermenting tree sap from the Uralic people, along with the word, and then transferred the word to another alcoholic drink once they started growing grain. But I don't know enough to say if this is a valid idea etymologically.

'Beer' is just as difficult to find a convincing etymology for. The *Oxford Dictionary of English Etymology* links it to the Old English word *beór*, and says it's from the Old High German *bior*, which gave the modern Dutch and German *bier* and tentatively suggests, 'perhaps from monastic Latin *biber*, drink,' an adoption of the Latin *bibere*. The (somewhat controversial) Russian linguist Vladimír Orel suggested bior was borrowed from a possible Romance (that is, the fissiparous language Latin became on its way to French, Spanish, Italian and so on) word **biw(e)r*, itself from Late Latin *biber*. In French, **biw(e)r* became *boire*, 'drink'. The big name behind this theory is Friedrich Kluge (1856–1926), who put forward the monastic Latin *biber* derivation for *bier* in his positively canonical *Etymologisches Wörterbuch der Deutschen Sprache*.

But there are several problems here. Old English had *beór*, Old Norse had *bjórr* and these must have been the equivalents of Old High German *bior*. However, as I showed earlier, Old English *beór* was probably not 'beer', but another kind of alcoholic drink, quite likely cider, and the same looks true of Old Norse *bjórr*. Nor is it clear where Old English *beór* and Old Norse *bjórr* came from. Not Romance, and not monastic Latin, probably: monasteries did not appear in Scandinavia until around the eleventh century, as far as I can see. *Beór* and *bjórr*, whatever they meant, disappear and Middle English and the Scandinavian languages carried on using 'ale' words for the fermented grain drink. At some point in the history of Old High German however, the old 'ale' word vanished, and *bier* was the word for fermented grain (hopped or unhopped, incidentally). Middle Dutch apparently still had *ael* or *ale* but this, too, eventually succumbed to bier. Why did Old High German *bior*, whatever it originally meant, push out the *al-* 'ale' word it had shared with Old English and Old Norse?

I have a theory, although this is almost pure speculation. I suspect that Old High German *bior* originally meant, as Old English *beór* seems to have done, an alcoholic drink but not 'ale'. In the many monasteries that sprang up across Germany in the sixth and seventh centuries, meanwhile, the Latin-speaking monks used *biber*, properly 'drink', to mean 'ale'. The Germans, in my piece of speculation, influenced by the similarity of *bior* and *biber*, then started widening the meaning of *bior* to encompass 'ale', and their original *al-* word disappeared.

But why did the monks use *biber* (a word with the same roots as 'imbibe') to mean 'ale' when Latin had a perfectly good word for ale, *cervisia*, derived from Celtic? More dangerous speculation, but many of the most influential monkish evangelists

in Germanic-speaking Europe during the sixth and seventh
centuries were Irish scholars and clerics, such as St Columbanus,
St Gall and St Kilian. Important centres of Irish-Christian
influence included Cologne, Mainz, Strasbourg, Salzburg and
Vienna, while St Kilian and his companions brought Christianity
to Franconia and Thuringia, and St Gall gave his name to an
important medieval monastery in modern Switzerland. In Irish,
the first language of these travelling saints, the word for ale,
as we have seen, had become *lionn*, which like *biber* originally
meant just 'drink'. Perhaps when Irish monks spoke in Latin
about *lionn*, meaning ale, they translated the word literally from
Irish into Latin as *biber*, 'drink', rather than *cervisia*, 'ale'.

That all contains too many 'ifs' to be likely, however, and
some even sneer anyway at Kluge's pushing forward *biber* as
the origin of 'beer'. Dr Joseph Garreau, professor emeritus of
French studies at the University of Massachussetts Lowell, calls
it 'wrong' and 'fanciful' to talk of the monks 'imbibing' their ale,
and insists instead that we look for the origins of the word 'beer'
in the Indo-European root **bher*, which expresses the idea of
bubbling, as in what happens both when liquids are boiled and
when yeast starts producing carbon dioxide as it creates alcohol.

*Bher is pretty definitely underneath a variety of brewing
words, including 'brew' itself, via pre-Germanic *breuh-e/o-*
(after what linguists call metathesis, the swapping of two
sounds, in this case 'r' and 'e'), then Proto-Germanic **brew-
i/a-* and on to Old English *brēowan*. Via Latin fervere, 'to boil'
(showing the regular change of 'b' to 'f' in Latin, as in the pair
'brother/*frater*') **bher* is behind the word 'fermentation'. It is
also the ultimate root for 'barm', an old word for yeast, via
Old English *beorma*, which is probably from a word in Proto-
Germanic or Old Teutonic (the language spoken in Scandinavia
in the first millennium BC from which all the modern Germanic
languages from Swedish to English are descended), hypothesised
as **bermon-*; the same word appears in both Danish and
modern German (or modern North German, anyway) as *bärme*,
'yeast', and in Swedish as *barma*. (And 'yeast' itself derives from
another Indo-European root word for 'boil', **ias-*.)

It even looks to have given us 'bride': in Proto-Germanic and some early German languages 'bride' (*brūths* in, for example, Gothic) seems to have originally meant 'daughter-in-law', from a root word derived again from **bher* and meaning 'to brew' and 'to cook, make broth' – the duties of a daughter-in-law, 2,000 and more years ago ('broth' itself being another word descended from **bher*). In modern German the connection appears even more obvious: *Braut* for 'bride', *Brauer* for 'brewer'.

The 'Garreau school' suggestion, as I understand it, is that Proto-Germanic **brew-i/a*, from **bher*, led to a Proto-West-Germanic **breura*, meaning the drink that is brewed, and from that, they claim, are derived Old High German *bior*, Old English *béor*, modern English 'beer' as an instance of 'loss of recurring phoneme'. In Thracian, the Indo-European language spoken just north of Greece from around 1000 BC until the fourth or fifth centuries AD, the word for beer, *brûtos* or *brytos*, certainly looks to be derived ultimately from **bher-*. *Brûtos*, then, was 'what has been brewed'. However, despite the example of Thracian, I'm less than convinced that the concept of bubbling, intimately connected with the action of yeast on sugary solutions, and with the act of brewing (and with boiling up broth) would have automatically attached itself to the drink. So 'brew' and 'barm' from **bher*, yes: 'beer' from **bher*, not so sure.

The third common explanation suggested for the origins of the word 'beer' link it to the word 'barley'. The name for the grain most commonly used today for brewing beer goes back to a likely Proto-Indo-European **b[h]ars-*, meaning 'grain' in general. Indeed, some linguists suggest Proto-Indo-European borrowed **b[h]ars-* from Proto-Semitic **barr-/*burr*, 'grain, cereal', which occurs today in Hebrew *bar*, 'grain', and Arabic *burr*, 'wheat'. This, at least, seems a sensible suggestion: both grain cultivation and (according to one theory) the Semitic languages developed in the Near East, and there are other agriculture-related borrowings from Proto-Semitic into Proto-Indo-European, including 'wine' (Proto-Semitic **wayn* > Proto-Indo-European **wóinom*).

In Proto-Germanic the word for barley has been hypothesised as developing from **b[h]ars-* to **beuwo-*, and the *Oxford*

English Dictionary suggests that possibly from this came an unrecorded Proto-Germanic word **beuro-*, 'drink made from **beuwo-*', out of which, perhaps, descended Old Norse *bjórr*, Old English *beór*, Old High German *bior* and so on down to 'beer'.

In the Scandinavian languages the '-w-' sound developed to '-gg-' (as in *bryggeri* = 'brewery'), so that **beuwo-* became *bygg* in Old Norse, which gives us English 'bigg', the name for a type of hardy four-row barley grown in Scotland (and in Scandinavia). In Old English **beuwo-* developed into *bere*. This is pronounced today the same as 'beer', and again, in the north of England and Scotland, it is used for a variety of coarse barley. This is enough to persuade some that bere, 'barley', is the root of 'beer' the drink. But *bere*, in the south of England, at least, was originally pronounced 'bar', as in 'barn', from '*bere aern*', 'barley house, place for storing barley', the place name Barton, from '*bere tun*', 'barley enclosure' and 'barley' itself, from '*bere-lic*', 'barley-like', that is, 'the grain similar to *bere*'. So that seems to rule out 'beer' coming from *bere*. Again, I'm no etymologist, but with no real evidence, I'm not convinced at all that **beuwo-*, 'barley' gave birth to a word that led to *bjórr/beór/bior*, 'beer'.

Overall, then, there's no compelling theory giving the origins of either 'ale' or 'beer' as words. 'Ale' certainly seems to be a mystery. If you find anyone stating as a fact that 'ale' or 'beer' definitely 'come from' any other word, then they're wrong. But with the examples of *pivo*, the word for beer in Slavic languages, and *lionn*, 'beer' in Modern Irish, which both originally just meant 'beverage' or 'drink' , I'm inclined to suspect that the roots of 'beer' lie in the Latin *bibere*, 'to drink', or a similar word also derived from the Proto-Indo-European base **po-/*pi-*, 'drink', even if the route wasn't via the monasteries of Germany. Using the general for the particular is common enough; if someone said to you, 'Fancy a drink?' you wouldn't assume they were thinking of sparkling mineral water.

25

What Did Pliny the Elder Say About Hops?

What did Pliny the Elder actually say about hops? Not what you've been told, probably – and quite possibly he said nothing about hops at all.

Thanks to the chaps at the Russian River brewery in Santa Rosa, Sonoma County, California, who named their highly regarded, extremely hoppy, strong 'double IPA' after him, the Roman author, lawyer and military man Gaius Minor Plinius Caecilius Secundus, known to us as Pliny – who died in AD 79 from a surfeit of scientific curiosity after getting too close to the exploding Mount Vesuvius and being suffocated by toxic fumes – is now probably better known than at any time in the past 1,900 years.

Russian River named the beer Pliny the Elder because he is supposed to be the first person to mention hops in writing, in his great survey of contemporary human knowledge, *Naturalis Historia*, or 'Natural History'. (They named an even hoppier, stronger 'triple IPA' after his nephew and heir, Pliny the Younger – and they also mispronounced Pliny, as 'Pl-eye-ni', instead of the proper 'Plinni'.)

But the plant that Pliny the Elder wrote about, which he said was called *lupus salictarius* (which translates as 'wolf of the willows', *salix* being the Latin for willow tree), may not have been the hop; there's certainly no completely convincing evidence in Pliny's own writings to confirm that *lupus salictarius* and hops are the same thing.

The first person to identify Pliny's *lupus salictarius* as the plant that Italians call *lupulo*, the Spanish *lúpulo*, Germans *Hopfen*

Picture of hops from a book by the sixteeth-century
Bavarian botanist Leonhart Fuchs, identifying them
as the *Lupus salictarius* of Pliny. But were they?

and English-speakers hops seems to have been a sixteenth-
century Bavarian botanist called Leonhart Fuchs, in a book
called *De historia stirpium commentarii insignes*, or *Notable
commentaries on the history of plants*. But Fuchs (after whom,
apparently, the fuchsia is named), had made a big effort to try
to match up 'modern' plants with those mentioned by classical
authors, and may have made a mistake in deciding that *lupulo*
was derived from, and identical with, Pliny's *lupus salictarius*.

At least one writer has suggested that the word *lupulo*, far from being derived from the earlier term, may simply be an Italian error for '*l'upulo*', via the French for hop, houblon, and nothing to do with *lupus salictarius*.

What did Pliny actually say about *lupus salictarius*? He mentions it, briefly, in book 21, chapter 50 of his *Natural History*, which is a short section about wild or uncultivated foods. After talking about the wild plants eaten in Egypt, he then says, '*In Italia paucissimas novimus, fraga, tamnum, ruscum, batim marinum, batim hortensiam, quam aliqui asparagum Gallicum vocant. Praeter has pastinacam pratensem, lupum salictarium, eaque verius oblectamenta quam cibos.*'

There are a number of translations of that passage around, many of which put words into Pliny's mouth that are not justified by the original. Here's my stab at an English version. 'In Italy there are only a few of these novelties: strawberries, black briony, butcher's broom, samphire, brambles, which some call Gallic asparagus. In addition there are wild parsnip and 'willow wolf', but these are really amusements rather than proper food.'

Now, we can take it (though Pliny doesn't specifically say so) that when he talks about eating plants such as black bryony (which is actually extremely poisonous, at least the berries, roots and leaves are), butcher's broom and brambles, he means eating the young springtime shoots. Young springtime hop shoots are still cooked and eaten in Belgium and elsewhere. But that doesn't prove that by *lupus salictarius* Pliny meant the hop.

What about the actual name *lupus salictarius*? You'll find plenty of people asserting that Pliny (more properly the Romans – Pliny didn't invent this name) called the hop 'willow wolf' 'because hops then grew wild among willows like a wolf in the forest', and a book from 1834 called *Medical Botany* by John Stephenson declares that 'according to Pliny [the hop] grew amongst willows, to which, by twining round, and choking them, it became as destructive as the wolf to the flock'. But, as we have seen, Pliny never said anything like this. The *Naturalis Historia* gives no explanation at all for the name *lupus salictarius*. Mr Stephenson et al. are making it up.

Now, as it happens, wild hops *will* (and do) climb up trees, and quite possibly in sufficient quantities to bring the trees down with their weight, the way wolves bring down sheep and other prey. I've not found any descriptions of this happening, although I've seen wild hops growing all over hedges in great quantities in England, and the botanist Humphrey Gilbert-Carter said, in his *Glossary of the British Flora* in 1949, that 'the hop is commonly seen climbing on the willow in the continental Auenwälder'. But that doesn't prove that *lupus salictarius* is the hop, either.

The biggest sceptic about the idea that *lupus salictarius* equals hop was Victor Hehn, author of a book called *The Wanderings of Plants and Animals from their First Home*, published in 1885. Hehn suggested that *lupulo* came from the Germanic *hoppe* via French.

> There arose a diminutive form out of this *hoppe* by the addition of an l, which explains the French *houblon* for *houbelon* as well as the Mid. Latin *hubalus*. Farther on, in Italy, where the plant was neither cultivated nor used, the foreign word, coalescing with the Article, became *lupolo, luppolo*; out of which popular name arose the later Mid. Latin *lupulus*, used by Italian authors. The botany of the Middle Ages was so slavishly dependent on the Graeco-Roman literature that a similar sounding name of a plant was hunted for and happily found in Pliny.

However, as Hehn says, in the very brief mention by Pliny of *lupus salictarius*, 'There is not a word about its being a climbing plant and if the name had not resembled the Mid. Latin *lupulus*, no one would have thought of its meaning the hop.'

Now, if you want my opinion (and I'm taking it that as you're reading this you *do* want my opinion), I think it's somewhere between possible and probable that *lupus salictarius* was the wild hop plant; Pliny puts it among other wild plants from which the fresh shoots were harvested for cooking, like asparagus, and hop shoots are still cooked today, while 'willow wolf' is a good description of what hops are capable of in the wild as they grow up trees for support. But that's a long way from 'definite', and to write as if Pliny's *lupus salictarius* was unequivocally the hop plant is wrong.

When the great Swedish botanist Carl von Linné, otherwise known as Linnaeus, attached a scientific name to the hop in 1753 he gave it the genus name *Humulus*, from the Swedish for 'hop', *humle*, and the species name *lupulus* from the medieval Latin word for 'hop'. Even if *lupus salictarius* were the origin of *lupulus*, therefore, it would be wrong to say, as many websites do, that Pliny 'is credited with inventing the botanical name for hops'. He didn't – Linnaeus did.

In fact there's a great deal of rubbish written about Pliny and hops on the interwebs; here's a brief cull.

'The Hop was first mentioned by Pliny, who speaks of it as a garden plant.' No he didn't. In fact he specifically put *lupus salictarius* in a section with other wild, uncultivated plants.

'Hops were used and consumed by Pliny the Elder and his Roman country men for medicinal purposes.' No they weren't.

'The hop was said by the Romans to grow wild among the willows "like a wolf among sheep."' No it wasn't.

'In the first century AD, Roman naturalist Pliny the Elder named the plant *Lupus salictarius* or "willow wolf" because of its habit of climbing up willow trees and strangling them.' No he didn't. Pliny didn't give *lupus salictarius* a name, he repeated the name others had given it earlier. We don't know why it was called 'willow wolf', we can only guess. Fortunately, none of that stops us enjoying hopped beers, and Russian River's Pliny the Elder, even if the name may be based on an error.

26

The Patron Saint of English Brewers

The patron saint of brewers is usually given as St Arnold of Flanders or his near-namesake St Arnould, bishop of Metz. But English brewers have their own (unofficial) saint, Thomas Becket, the Archbishop of Canterbury who was assassinated in the twelfth century in his own cathedral by four knights acting on the supposed instructions of King Henry II.

Thomas was born in or about 1118 – quite probably on 21 December, St Thomas the Apostle's Day – in a house in Cheapside, London, between streets that are today called Ironmonger Lane and Old Jewry. His father, Gilbert, a wealthy former merchant and property owner, was born in the village of Thierville in Normandy. Whether Becket was the family name, or a nickname given to Thomas, sources disagree; in his own lifetime Thomas called himself 'Thomas of London'. (The style Thomas à Becket, incidentally, seems not to have been used until after the Reformation.)

In 1139 Theobald of Bec, who was also from the Thierville area, became Archbishop of Canterbury, and his patronage undoubtedly helped the young Thomas of London. However, the thirteenth-century historian Matthew Paris, a monk at St Alban's Abbey in Hertfordshire, said Thomas was given his first post in the Church by the Abbot of St Alban's, Geoffrey de Gorron (or Gorham). Geoffrey supposedly made the young Thomas the priest at St Andrew's church, Bramfield, a small village about five miles north of Hertford, an appointment some historians say took place in or around 1142.

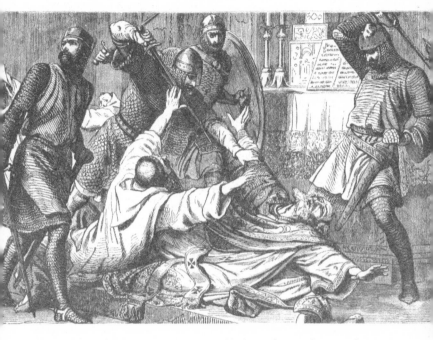

The murder of Thomas Becket – archbishop, former brewer, former Chancellor and later saint – at Canterbury Cathedral in 1170, from a book published in Switzerland in 1877. (British Library)

While at Bramfield, its village historians claim, Thomas brewed ale using water from the old vicarage pond. This was described in the nineteenth century as 'a little bricked-in muddy pond in the vicarage farmyard', and it is still known as Becket's pool or Becket's pond. If this sounds unhygienic (particularly as tradition also says Becket and his monks used to wash in the pool), using pond water to brew ale and beer was a very common practice. The farmer-diarist John Carrington, whose son ran the Rose and Crown at the nearby village of Tewin, took water from his farm pond at Bramfield to make his harvest ale with as late as 1800. The village clerics also drank home-brewed ale for hundreds of years – one history of Bramfield says the vicar still brewed his own beer until the nineteenth century.

Unfortunately for Bramfield, other sources put Thomas as a student in Paris from the mid-1130s or so until around 1140 or 1142, not in Hertfordshire. After that, it is said, he then worked in London as a clerk for a kinsman with the wonderful name of Osbert Huitdeniers, or Ossie Eightpence. Osbert seems to have been what passed in the twelfth century as a banker. By 1146 Thomas had won a place in the household of Archbishop Theobald as a clerk, presumably through his father Gilbert's Thierville connections (Gilbert had apparently, by this time, lost all his wealth, possibly in a fire). As evidence in favour of the Bramfield connection, however, shortly before Thomas was killed in the cathedral at Canterbury, he is said to have reminded the then Abbot of St Alban's that it was his monastery that gave Thomas of London his first 'honour' – the 'ecclesiola' ('little church)' at Bramfield – when he was young and poor.

It is quite possible Thomas was given the appointment – and with it the priestly income – when he was working for Theobald, but that a deputy stood in for him to perform the actual duties of the priest at Bramfield. On the other hand, after Thomas's assassination, when he was made a saint, a Saxon well at Bramfield church was renamed the Holy Well of St Thomas and attracted pilgrims for its reputed healing powers, again suggesting a close connection between the saint and the village.

In 1154, after six or more years in Theobald's service, Thomas was appointed by the Archbishop as archdeacon of Canterbury, a post worth around £100 a year. This was a substantial sum in twelfth century England, equivalent to perhaps £80,000 a year today, and showed that Thomas, now in his mid-thirties, was highly regarded by the archbishop. His new post did not last long, and he had clearly impressed the right people; just a few months later the newly crowned Henry II, then only twenty-one, pulled Thomas from the Archbishop's staff and made him Chancellor, one of the most powerful positions in the kingdom.

For eight years Henry and Thomas worked together, developing a close friendship. At one point, in 1158, Thomas visited France on Henry's behalf to demand the hand of the French king's daughter for the English king's eldest son (who was only three – though the sought-after bride herself was just a few months old). Thomas took with him a deliberately extravagant cavalcade designed to proclaim the glories of England. It included 250 footmen singing anthems in English, twenty-eight packhorses bearing gold and silver plate, English-bred mastiffs, greyhounds and hawks, grooms holding monkeys dressed in English livery and, according to a widely-quoted passage supposedly from a contemporary chronicler, two chariots 'laden solely with iron-bound barrels of ale, decocted from choice, fat grain, as a gift for the French, who wondered at such an invention, a drink most wholesome, clear of all dregs, rivalling wine in colour and surpassing it in flavour'.

The passage is significant in suggesting that ale before hops could travel, and could keep the fortnight or more it must have taken in the twelfth century to get from England to the French king's court. It also shows that, on special occasions at least, ale casks in the twelfth century were hooped with metal.

In 1162, Thomas was appointed by Henry II to be Archbishop of Canterbury, soon after the death of Thomas's patron, Theobald. Undoubtedly Henry made Thomas archbishop because he wanted an ally in the second-most-important position in England. However, to Henry's certain amazement and anger, Thomas immediately put himself in opposition to the king's policies. The two began quarrelling by the following year, and in November 1164 Thomas left the country, having been found guilty at a meeting of the great council at Northampton Castle of contempt of royal authority and malfeasance in the chancellor's office. However, anyone who stood up to kings was inevitably popular with the ordinary people, and when the archbishop returned to England in 1170 he was greeted with acclaim. It was this that probably most got up King Henry's royal nose, and led to four knights, supposedly acting on what they believed to be the king's orders, murdering Thomas in the cathedral at Canterbury on 29 December 1170.

Within three years, the former Bramfield brewer was canonised – the pope in Rome naturally wanting to send a message to kings who had archbishops bumped off. Thomas's shrine at Canterbury, built in the reign of Henry III in 1220, became one of the most popular destinations for pilgrims. Their usual journey started from Southwark, where Becket had delivered a sermon at St Mary's Priory, now the Cathedral, six days before his death, with the pilgrims retracing the saint's last trip across Kent. Although one account of Thomas's life says he had a weak stomach, and could not drink wine or ale, the members of the Brewer's Company in London claimed their saintly fellow Londoner as the guild's founder, with roots supposedly in the late twelfth century as the 'Guild of Our Lady and St Thomas Becket'. When the London brewers received their first charter in the fifteenth century, their organisation was known as the Guild of St Mary and St Thomas the Martyr. In 1468, the brewers were awarded their own armorial bearings. They honoured their supposed links with the saint by impaling the traditional brewer's three tuns and barley sheaves alongside the armorial insignia of St Thomas, the Becket family's three ravens or choughs, birds also known as 'beckets', and the arms of the Archbishop of Canterbury.

However, seventy years later, in 1538, another King Henry, Henry VIII, declared Becket to have been a traitor; his shrine at Canterbury was destroyed, his bones burned and his name removed from the service books. He also insisted that all churches dedicated to St Thomas the Martyr had to be renamed. Henry VIII was having his own problems with the Church (and chancellors called Thomas – Thomas Cromwell, himself the son of a brewer from Putney), and did not want any reminders of clerics who had defied kings. The next year, 1539, the City of London, which has St Thomas the Martyr and St Paul as its joint official saints, took the image of Thomas off its seal. The brewers hung on a little longer, but eventually, in 1543/4, decided it would be smart politics to take Becket's arms off theirs and acquire a new set.

In their new arms the brewers still managed to sneak in a subtle reference to Thomas, however. To this day the crest of the Brewers' Company shows a dark-skinned woman with fair hair, a nod to the (inaccurate) tradition that St Thomas's mother was a Saracen who had followed his father Gilbert home from the Crusades. It is lucky Bluff King Hal never realised what the brewers and the heralds were up to, in still maintaining a link to a banned saint; one estimate says that Henry VIII had 75,000 people killed during his reign. A few cheeky brewers added to the list would not have worried him.

27

The Jerusalem Tavern, the Trigger's Broom of Pubs

The Jerusalem Tavern at 55 Britton Street, Clerkenwell, EC1, many people's favourite London pub, is like one of those old knives that have had two new handles and three new blades. From one direction it is one of London's ancient hostelries; its roots lie back in the Crusades, and the Priory of St John of Jerusalem, which dominated Clerkenwell until the time of Elizabeth I. Looked at from another direction, however, the pub is a young pretender just coming out of its teens.

The Jerusalem Tavern's interior, with its worn green-painted settles, dark oak floorboards, old tiles set in the walls and ceilings the colour of well-smoked kippers, certainly looks as if Samuel Johnson might pop in any moment from his job as a freelance writer round the corner at the offices of the *Gentlemen's Magazine* to meet the poet Oliver Goldsmith for a refreshing quart of porter. However, it has only been licensed premises since 1996: this pub is younger than most of the people who drink in it.

The building is authentically early Georgian, though, and Johnson might well have passed by on his way to work. It was built in 1719/20 as one of a group of townhouses on a piece of open ground that had originally belonged to the Priory of St John of Jerusalem, which had stood nearby. The new street was then, and for the next couple of hundred years, called Red Lion Street, after a tavern at the top of the road, on Clerkenwell Green. The developer was a lawyer called Simon Michell, MP for Boston, whose father was from Somerset, and the Red Lion

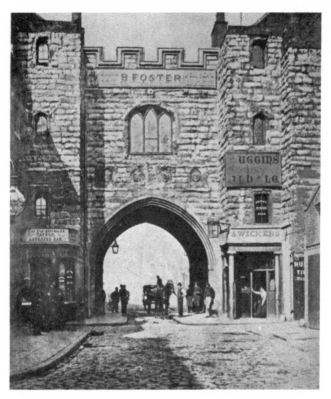

The Jerusalem Tavern in its third incarnation, around 1860, when it occupied St John's Gate, the former main gateway to the Priory of St John of Jerusalem in Clerkenwell, London. (Author's collection)

Street homes were reckoned to be 'the best class of houses erected in his time in Clerkenwell'.

Around 1810, a shop front was inserted into the façade of Number 55, and the premises became a watchmaker's; Clerkenwell was a centre of watchmaking from around or before the start of the eighteenth century, and there were several watchmakers in the street. Over the years, Number 55 has had a variety of occupants; from 1952 it was the headquarters of a book publishing company, Burke & Co, and in the 1980s it was used as an architect's offices by a man called Oliver Bland.

In 1992, it was bought by a man called Julian Humphreys, who redesigned the ground floor as a recreation of an eighteenth-century coffee house, installing the panelling, the pews, the Delft tiles and the scrubbed floor we see today. The premises ran from January 1995 to August 1996, under the name The Jerusalem Coffee House, a nod to the former priory, after which Humphreys leased it to the newly opened St Peter's Brewery of Bungay in Suffolk for 25 years. The brewery had been started by John Murphy, the founder of the branding consultancy Interbrand (which gave the world the Hobnob biscuit, *inter alia*). Humphreys suggested to Murphy that he rename the place the Jerusalem Tavern, a name long associated with the area; four other Jerusalem Taverns have operated within three hundred yards of the present pub, though the most recent predecessor closed around a century ago.

The original Jerusalem Tavern, in full the St John of Jerusalem Tavern, was a short walk east of Clerkenwell Green, on the top right-hand or north-east corner of Jerusalem Passage at it enters Aylesbury Street. The blasting through of Clerkenwell Road in 1878 has wrecked the ancient geography of this section of London, but Jerusalem Passage was originally the street that led to the 'Little Gate of St John', the northern entrance into the Priory of St John of Jerusalem (the saint otherwise known as John the Baptist).

The priory was founded in the 1140s on five acres of donated land just outside the City of London that stretched, as far as I have been able to ascertain, from the present-day St John Street down to the Fleet river. It was the local branch of an international order of Knights Hospitallers, which had its roots in Jerusalem in the middle or so of the eleventh century, and which became a formal organisation in 1099. The Knights, who originally wore black cloaks marked with a white cross, were eventually pushed out of the Holy Land, and the Near East, by the soldiers of Islam. They were granted a home on Malta by the Holy Roman Emperor, Charles V, with a rent to be paid to the King of Spain of one falcon a year (which gave Dashiell Hammett the idea for the story of *The Maltese Falcon*).

Back in England, the Clerkenwell priory, including its great mansion house, had been burnt to the ground in 1381 during the Peasants' Revolt, and its prior, Sir Robert Hales, beheaded by the rebels for his part (as Lord High Treasurer) in imposing the hated poll tax. It bounced back, and early in the sixteenth century, in 1504, a substantial south gate was erected to guard St John's Lane by the then prior, Sir Thomas Docwra. However, in 1540 Henry VIII added the priory to his general nationalisation of church property; it was a wealthy institution, owning, for example, St John's Wood (now in West London, which is, of course, named after the priory), and having an income of two or three thousand pounds a year. Although Henry's eldest daughter, Mary, had it opened again, under Elizabeth I it closed for good and most of the priory buildings, except for the south gate, were gradually demolished.

It ought to be possible to declare that the St John of Jerusalem Tavern at the top of Jerusalem Passage, just outside the priory's north gate, was in existence during at least some of the four centuries that the Priory of St John of Jerusalem was operating as the English base of the Knights Hospitallers. Its description as a tavern, a name originally restricted, in medieval England, solely to those places licensed to sell wine, hints at an ancient establishment. The priory (which, incidentally, like most or all religious houses, brewed its own ale: one year it used 225 quarters of oats in brewing) was a popular place for the nobility to stay when they were visiting London, and guests over the centuries included King John, the future Edward I and Henrys IV and V. At least some of those retainers who accompanied the royal guests and other noble travellers lodging at the priory must have looked to slip out for a quick Gascon red or Rhenish white, and the tavern, if it existed then, would have been perfectly placed to supply their wants.

Certainly, religious houses and taverns went together. The nearby Charterhouse monastery off Smithfield, owned by the monks of the Carthusian order, had four taverns just outside the monastery walls, which were supplied with water from the monastery. It seems perfectly possible that the St John of Jerusalem Tavern bore the same relationship to the Priory of St John that those four taverns bore to the Charterhouse. There was another old tavern on the south side of the priory, in St John's Lane, the Old Baptist's Head (which seems to have inspired the signboard of the current Jerusalem Tavern), which only closed around 1944. Its name, too, suggests an intimate link with the priory, making, potentially, a pair of taverns just outside the priory walls to match the four outside the walls of the Charterhouse monastery.

However, there appears to be no evidence for asserting that either of these two drinking places were open when the priory was in its pomp. The Old Baptist's Head does not seem to have existed as a tavern before the seventeenth century, and the earliest mention I have been able to find for the Jerusalem Tavern is from October 1692, when the Middlesex justices were ordering that the road (now Aylesbury Street) between the St John of Jerusalem Tavern and St John Street be paved with stone. Less than seventy years later, in 1758, the tavern was pulled down so that Clerkenwell Parish Schools could be built on the site.

Immediately after the St John of Jerusalem was demolished, William Newell, the landlord of the Red Lion on Clerkenwell Green that had given its name to Simon Michell's Red Lion Street, rechristened his premises the Jerusalem Tavern: in 1759 the *London Chronicle* recorded that the annual 'Feast of the Cockneys' (there's an event I'd like to see revived) had been held at the Jerusalem Tavern, with singing by the St Paul's cathedral choir, the money raised going to the new parish schools. Very probably Newell was encouraged to change the name of his pub because of the existence of several other Red Lions in the area, including one in St John Street to the east and one in Holborn to the west.

Newell died soon after the renaming (his widow remarried in 1762), but the Jerusalem Tavern continued without him. It was a meeting-place for the local Freemasons' Lodge, and in 1769 they showed their support for the kind of radical politics Clerkenwell has often been known for by electing John Wilkes (born in

Clerkenwell, where his father owned a gin distillery) a member of the Lodge, though he was in prison at the time for upsetting the government of George III. This second Jerusalem Tavern was known for supplying fine wines, as a tavern should be. In 1787 a sixteen-year-old Wiltshire lad called John Britton was apprenticed by his uncle to the tavern's owner, Mr T. Mendham, as cellar boy. Britton later achieved fame as a virtually self-taught antiquarian and expert in architecture and topography who would be involved in the authoring, jointly or on his own, of almost a hundred books. The six years he spent working in the Jerusalem Tavern were honoured in 1936 when Red Lion Street was named after him, to stop the confusion with other Red Lion Streets nearby.

It looks as if the second Jerusalem Tavern closed sometime soon after 1794, and the name was transferred again, this time to premises actually in the east turret of the still-standing south gate of the priory. In 1731, St John's Gate had become the offices of the newly launched *Gentleman's Magazine*, where Samuel Johnson worked from 1738 to around 1745. The magazine moved to Fleet Street in 1787. Its then part-owner, David Henry, had married William Newell's widow: it seems more than possible that this connection had something to do with part of St John's Gate becoming the new Jerusalem Tavern. Exactly when the third incarnation of the Jerusalem Tavern started is unclear, but it was certainly in place by 1801, when an Old Bailey court case featured a man arrested for trying to sell a counterfeit seven-shilling piece to a policeman at the Jerusalem Tavern, St John's Gate.

The tavern had a tendency to vary its name. In 1825 it is referred to as 'The old St John of Jerusalem', 'occupied and kept by Mr William Flint, who formerly carried on the business of a printer in the Old Bailey'. (There was another St John of Jerusalem in St John Street, north of Aylesbury Street, which was running by around 1839 and only closed in 1992.)

In 1845 St John's Gate, by now literally dilapidated, was condemned as being dangerous, and it was proposed to demolish the building. However, a public fund was started to raise the money to repair and embellish it, and over the next two years the stonework was replaced and the crenellation along the top, which had disappeared sometime in the previous 180 years, was restored, all at a total cost of 'upwards of £130'.

From 1848, the landlord of the Jerusalem Tavern was Benjamin Foster, and his name appears on the signboard in a photograph of the gateway taken around 1860. The tavern's porter was supplied by Reid's, one of the biggest London porter brewers. Reid's brewery was a short distance to the west across the Fleet, in Liquorpond Street (one of several streets that disappeared when the Clerkenwell Road was built). The ale at the Jerusalem Tavern came from Huggins's brewery in Broad Street (now Broadwick Street), off Golden Square, near what is now Piccadilly Circus.

Foster was an antiquarian manqué, and it was said of him in 1858 that 'a great portion of the interior of the tavern has lately been restored to its original state by Mr Foster at a considerable expense'. It may have been Foster who started the annual 'Boar's Head Feast' every Christmas at the Jerusalem Tavern, which was still going in 1869. It was probably Foster who declared that an old chair found on the premises was the very one that Dr Johnson had sat in when he was writing for the *Gentleman's Magazine*. Hmm. Walter Thornbury, writing in 1872, said of Foster that after he arrived at the Jerusalem Tavern, he 'hunted up traditions of the place, and, indeed, where they were thin, invented them'. Foster actually wrote a book on *Ye History of Ye Priory and Gate of St John*, published in 1851. He died of apoplexy in 1863 and was apparently followed at the Jerusalem Tavern by his son-in-law.

In 1873 a revived version of the Order of the Hospital of St John of Jerusalem regained ownership of the priory's south gate, and in 1876 the Jerusalem Tavern apparently moved to newly built premises alongside the gate. (The following year, the Order founded the St John Ambulance Association, which still has its Secretariat at St John's Gate.) The Jerusalem Tavern appears to have continued running until the First World War, but it looks as if this fourth incarnation finally closed about 1915.

A fair degree of misinformation has grown up around the tangled history of the Jerusalem Tavern, much of it linked to Thomas Britton, the so-called 'musical small-coal man', who lived, until his death in 1714, on the opposite side of Jerusalem Passage to the original Jerusalem Tavern. Despite his trade as a coal-seller he was a self-taught musician, who founded a music club in Jerusalem Passage that attracted the likes of the composer Handel, among other distinguished visitors. At least one specialist book on London street names claims, wrongly, that Britton Street is named after Thomas, and others have asserted that Handel and other guests of Thomas Britton's musical events at his home in Jerusalem Passage were patrons of the original Jerusalem Tavern opposite. Possibly they were, but there is no evidence for it. There are even websites that, apparently totally confused, seem to think the current Jerusalem Tavern has been licensed premises since 1720.

That anyone could think it was a genuine 300-year-old pub is a tremendous credit to Julian Humphreys' original coffee-shop design from 1995, and to John Murphy and his team for maintaining it. The Jerusalem Tavern shows you can give a new pub character; the fastidious might wish to condemn it as fake, but I include myself as one of its very many fans, and I'm pleased whenever I have an excuse to call in for a pint of St Peter's: I always hope they have porter available, so that I can sip the black stuff and imagine I'm waiting for Samuel Johnson, wig awry, breeches shiny from sitting on a chair all day, to call in on his way home.

28

The Nettle and the Damage Done

One of the joys of being a beer writer is that occasionally nice brewers send me beer through the post. The only hitch is that some courier companies are a cretinous collection of cack-handed clowns, which means that when the package finally arrives, it won't necessarily be in the state it was when it left the brewery. Surprise was absent, therefore, when on one occasion I picked up a parcel that Hall and Woodhouse, owners of the Badger brewery in Dorset, had sent me via Britain's least-favourite delivery company and heard the sound of broken glass from inside.

Happily, the courier company had let itself down badly and smashed only one bottle, plus the half-pint glass that accompanied the beers, while, in the three attempts it made to deliver the package to me, the spilt beer had dried out. Even more happily, the two bottles of Stinger, H&W's organic brew made, in part, with nettles (can you get unorganic nettles?), were still intact.

Humanity has been good for nettles, so it's unkind of them to repay us by stinging so painfully. The plants need soils rich in phosphates, and, as Richard Mabey wrote in his marvellous book *Flora Britannica*, 'Human settlements provide phosphates in abundance, in cattle-pens, middens, bonfire sites, refuse dumps and churchyards.' Even long-abandoned human habitations continue to have nettles growing around them when there might not be any other nettles for miles. According to Mabey, 'the wooded sites of Romano-British villages on the Grovely Ridge near Salisbury are still dense with nettles subsisting on the remains of an occupation that ended 1,600 years ago.'

The Roman word for nettle was *urtica*, from which comes the modern botanical name for the stinging nettle, *urtica dioica*. Many books on herbs will try to tell you, wrongly, that *urtica* is derived from '*uro*', 'I burn' in Latin. This is the same sort of false Latin folk etymology that tried to derive *cerevisia*, the Roman word for beer, from Ceres, the Roman goddess of the harvest. Dictionaries prefer to say that *urtica* is 'o. o. o.' – that's 'of obscure origin', rather than the sound you make if you fall in a nettle-patch. Nettles are related, botanically, to hemp and hops; botanists still regard the three plants as monophylitic, that is, descended from one common ancestor, along with elder trees, mulberries and figs, and they used to put them all in an order called the Urticales. Since 2003, however, after DNA studies brought a truer picture of their descent, the 'Urticales' have been subsumed into the order Rosales, along with a large number of other plants and trees, including roses, apples, strawberries, almonds and peaches.

Perhaps because prehistoric farmers found nettles rapidly colonising the land around their settlements, which meant no travelling was required to gather them, they were used as a resource in a variety of ways. Neolithic settlements in Switzerland have provided evidence that nettle fibre was spun into cloth before either linen or wool; the fibres of nettle stalks, when processed, make a strong, pure-white thread that was used for fishing nets and fishing lines, as well as cloth. Maude Grieve's book *A Modern Herbal* says nettle fibres were still used to make sheets and tablecloths in Scotland in the sixteenth and seventeenth centuries (which looks to be true, though other claims Grieve makes, such as the etymology of the word 'nettle', are far off target).

When Neolithic farmers were gathering nettles to make cloth, they were left with piles of stripped-off leaves, the inspiration, Jacqui Wood suggests, in her book *Prehistoric Cooking*, for a wide range of dishes with nettle leaves in them. These include creamed nettles, cooked like spinach; fried nettles; nettle oatcakes; and boiled nettle pudding. In the spring, after a winter without fresh vegetables, nettle dishes would have been very welcome: young nettles are an excellent source of Vitamin C, as well as mineral salts. (The liquid that nettles have been boiled in, Wood says, incidentally, makes an excellent antiseptic for bathing cuts – and nettle juice also makes a good green dye.)

Boiled nettles can also be used instead of rennet to curdle milk for cheese-making; one variety of nettle cheese in the seventeenth century was called Slipcoat cheese, and was made by leaving the salted, drained, inch-thick curd to lie on nettle leaves for eight days, changing the leaves every day.

Other dishes containing nettles include nettle soup (regarded as 'famine food' in the Saxon era, though later versions include potatoes, chicken stock and cream). C. Anne Wilson, in *Food and Drink in Britain*, suggests nettles were used as potherbs in England up to the seventeenth century, while 'Scottish highlanders scorned garden plants and plucked nettles for their pottage'. Roger Phillips's *Wild Food* says nettles were grown under glass in Scotland as 'early kale', and the wild variety was popular in broths, porridge and haggis. In Ireland, Phillips says, 'A broth of water, nettles, salt, milk and oatmeal, called *Brotchan Neanntog,* was a favourite Irish dish until the cabbage became popular less than 200 years ago. Many of the poorer people still relied on *Brotchan Neanntog* to a considerable extent in the earlier part of the twentieth century.'

The brewing of nettle beer, while every commentator agrees it went on, is mostly unrecorded as far as the details go, probably because it was strictly a rural activity carried out by the poor and illiterate. But most versions miss out both hops and malt. Roger Phillips has a recipe for nettle beer, which looks to date back at least to the nineteenth century, and which used 100 nettle stalks, with leaves, and 3 lb of sugar to 2.5 gallons of water. Another recipe, collected by Cindy Renfrow from a book published in 1925, requires 'half a peck' (enough to fill a gallon bucket) of nettles to 2 lb of sugar and 5 gallons of water. C. J. J. Berry, one of the fathers of modern home brewing in Britain, has the only recipe I have found using malt and hops: 2 gallons of nettles, 4 lb of malt, 1.5 lb of sugar, 2oz of hops, and ginger, lemons and sarsaparilla too. Berry claims that nettles 'were once used in making stouts', though he gives no source.

Stephen Harrod Buhner, the American beer writer, describes nettle beer as 'one of the sublime herb beers. The taste really is indescribable, being a blend of a number of flavours, a veritable gustatory extravaganza'. He is probably in a minority, however. I was lucky enough, about 1996, to have a pint of what must be one of the very few draught nettle beers ever commercially-produced. It was made by one of the former Firkin chain of home-brew pubs in London as a springtime one-off to a recipe supplied, as I recall, by the uncle of the brewer. It was a hop-free beer with a green, herby taste, very pleasant once you accepted it for what it was, but different enough that the bartender in the Frigate and Firkin, behind Earls Court, insisted anyone trying it for the first time had an initial small glass to see if they wanted to go on for more.

One of the few other commercial unhopped nettle beers was the St Peter's Brewery's King Cnut, a development of their Millennium ale, made by the Suffolk-based brewery for the Millennium celebrations in 2000 to replicate the ales of a thousand years earlier. King Cnut, however, contained juniper berries, a Scandinavian tradition but not a British one, and for me the juniper was too much at the front. However, the beer seems to have disappeared from the St Peter's range.

That nettle beer I was sent was made after Hall and Woodhouse teamed up with the television chef and restaurateur Hugh Fearnley-Whittingstall, who was evidently getting in touch with his brewing roots (his nineteenth-century ancestor Edmund Fearnley, a 'beast salesman' at Smithfield market in London, changed his surname after inheriting a brewery in Watford from a Mr Whittingstall), to brew a beer with nettles that had been gathered from Hugh's farm in Dorset. It was a 4.5 per cent abv beer, dry-hopped with Challenger, Target and Styrian Goldings hops, and the hops were certainly well-forward in the flavour, with the nettles a green and slightly mysterious presence in the background, like a Wild Man of the Woods lurking on the edge of the picture.

Sadly, that beer seems to have disappeared now from the brewery's range, although at the last time of looking it was still making a draught nettle beer called Billy Stinger. The original version made an excellent table beer, though I didn't agree with Hugh Fearnley-Whittingstall's own suggestion that Stinger was 'good with ... winter roasts'. Roast chicken, yes, roast pork perhaps, but beef would have swamped the subtlety that the nettles brought to the brew, and most roasts need a more caramelly ale than this was. One excellent set of matches would be with soft cheeses, and crumbly cheeses such as Wensleydale, where the herby flavours have a chance to show off. It would also be fun to drink nettle beer with nettle dishes – fried nettles, creamed nettles, or (and here I'm definitely starting to feel hungry) a pork or salmon roulade with nettles instead of sage.